GREG MILLER'S GREATEST
WHITETAIL
ADVENTURES

BY GREG MILLER

Published by

krause
publications
The World's Largest Hobby & Collectibles Publisher

Please call or write for a free catalog of publications.
The toll-free number to place an order or to request a
free catalog is (800) 258-0929, or use our regular
business number (715) 445-2214.
Library of Congress Catalog Number: 2001096285
ISBN: 0-87349-382-6
Printed in the United States of America

Photography by Greg Miller

To the many deer hunters who, like me,
consider the importance of the kill
secondary to the quality of the hunt.

Contents

Introduction

I remember well one of my greatest childhood passions. I would sit upstairs in our den with my nose buried in the pages of Outdoor Life, Field & Stream and Sports Afield. That was during the 1960s, when those publications were filled with firsthand accounts of hunting and fishing adventures. (Sadly, the "Big Three" seldom run such stories nowadays.)

I considered myself lucky. Because of my dad's love for reading well-written adventure articles, he refused to let my mother throw away any of his hunting magazines. The result was a stockpile of great reading material that dated back to the mid-1950s.

Names such as O'Connor, Annabel and Dalrymple were as familiar and sacred to me as the names of some relatives. Those guys didn't just write stories; they had the talent to take me on their hunts to Africa's bush veldt, the mountains of Alaska or the southern Texas brush country. For someone who loved to hunt as much as me, it was a magical experience.

Unfortunately, adventure-type articles have all but disappeared. However, you can't blame magazines for that trend. They changed their slant to accommodate the desires of readers. During the 1980s and early 1990s, the demand for "how-to" articles exceeded the demand for adventure stories.

But I've noticed a trend recently. People often tell me they would rather read a good adventure article than a how-to piece. As one guy said: "I much prefer to read articles about people who just go out hunting. It doesn't matter if they kill something or not, as long as the stories are good. Anyone who hunts can relate to those kind of articles."

I've long thought about writing a book about some of my deer hunting adventures. Unfortunately, the demand for how-to material kept me from doing that. Further, I couldn't justify spending time on a project that might be doomed.

But I believe people want a break from the glut of run-of-the-mill how-to stories. Also, to confirm that market existed, I've asked dozens of hunters if they would buy a deer hunting adventure book. Most said they would.

I don't consider myself in the league of O'Connor or Annabel, and I don't possess their storytelling skills. However, I have a wealth of cherished deer hunting memories, and it's time I share some.

Almost every hunt in this book has been mentioned in one of my articles or a chapter from one of my previous books. However, because I've had to adhere to strict word counts in those articles and chapters, I've seldom told the entire story behind some of my most memorable adventures. Now, for the first time, you can read about those hunts from beginning to end.

I must mention one thing: I didn't write this book to brag about my deer hunting accomplishments. If that were true, I would only have written the stories behind my largest whitetails. This book is more about memories and less about antler size.

I realize many hunters would feel cheated if they read a deer hunting book and didn't learn anything. I learned valuable lessons from every hunt mentioned in this book, and I'll discuss those in detail at the end of each chapter.

Come on, let's go chase some whitetails!

The Axehandle Buck

A heavy snow was falling during a Friday afternoon in mid-November 1966. I stood with five other young bow-hunters from my home town of Bloomer, Wis., watching with great interest. The early bow season would close after the weekend, and we couldn't imagine a better way to finish than fresh tracking snow and rutting bucks.

My friends and I started planning our hunt during lunch hour, and we met again after school to apply the finishing touches. We decided to arrive at one of our favorite stomping grounds before daylight Saturday morning. The area was near Axehandle Lake, about 12 miles north of Bloomer. Group members included me, my brother Mike, Richie Berg, Bill Bucholtz, and Paul and "Rabs" Gumness.

None of us were old enough to drive, but that had never stopped us from hunting. Bill's father, "Bucky," was always willing to drive us to hunting spots and pick us up at the end of the day. He had only one requirement.

"You guys had better be waiting for me at the meeting spot when I get there, or you can find your own way home," Bucky always said sternly.

We never argued, but we never really worried about his threats, either. We knew from experience that, regardless of how late we were, Bucky would always be waiting at the meeting spot.

Young but Not Intimidated

The Axehandle Lake area remained a virtual wilderness in the mid-1960s. You could walk long distances in almost any direction without hitting a road. Huge tracts of hardwood forests were interspersed with many thick, wet swamps. It was the kind of country that could intimidate older, more-experienced hunters. Amazingly, however, none of us gave it a second thought. We would plunge into the woods before dawn and, often, not leave until daylight was fading. We were so busy hunting and having fun that we didn't worry about little things like getting lost.

It wasn't just youthful enthusiasm that prevented us from feeling intimidated. Though we were relatively inexperienced bow-hunters, we knew the lay of the land from countless hours of walking in the woods. I'd like to say the primary reason for those trips was to scout for deer sign and seek promising stand sites, but that wasn't true. We just liked to be in the woods year-round.

Even so, our time afield taught us several things about deer, such as where they fed, watered and hid during daylight. We also knew where deer traveled most. That knowledge led to many encounters with whitetails during those early years.

Long on Desire, Short on Ability

However, we quickly learned there was a huge difference between getting near deer and shooting them. Our inability to close the deal wasn't because we weren't proficient archers. We had shot hundreds of arrows at the practice range, and we were fairly deadly to 20 yards. Our abilities rapidly decreased beyond that, however.

Unlike some bow-hunters of that era, we knew a couple of area archery dealers. Buying cedar arrows, Bear and Zwickey broadheads, and Bear, Herter's and Ben Pearson bows wasn't a problem. I carried a Ben Pearson fiberglass recurve my first season, and then bought a used Bear Kodiak laminated recurve before my second season. I carried that bow until I entered the Air Force in 1970. I cherished that bow and wish I had kept it.

We'd each had encounters with whitetails and, by rights, should have killed at least one deer during those early years. But before that November 1966 morning, we hadn't cut a hair. The main rea-

It wasn't just youthful enthusiasm that kept us from being intimidated by the big woods. We were also familiar with our hunting area.

son wasn't a mystery, either. We suffered from the same affliction our fathers had: buck fever.

I still remember the loss of control I experienced every time a deer came within 20 yards. I would hear my heart pounding in my ears. My breath came in rapid gulps, and I would shake so badly that my arrow usually fell off the rest. Unbelievably, deer sometimes stood and watched as I self-destructed. That only made me more nervous. I was a basket case when I got my arrow back on the rest and came to full draw. Usually, my arrow whizzed harmlessly over the deer's back. It typically took me 10 minutes to recover, and even then, my knees were weak. Gosh, how I loved it!

I don't think anyone in our group had much hope that one of our arrows would eventually find the mark. But Bucky did, and he constantly encouraged us to keep hunting.

"You guys are getting shots just about every time you go out," he said. "One of these times, it's all going to come together, and

Mike and I hadn't been in the woods long when we jumped some deer. For lack of a better plan, we began trailing the whitetails.

somebody's going to hit a deer. It's just a matter of time."

Deer Ahead of Us

Saturday morning dawned clear and cold. Three inches of fresh snow blanketed the ground. Bucky drove us 12 miles to our hunting spot and dropped us off. We were preparing to head into the woods when Bucky rolled down his window and issued instructions.

"You guys better be waiting for me right here at dark or you'll have to find your own way back to Bloomer," he said.

We assured him we would be waiting and waved goodbye.

We had a brief meeting and chose a spot to meet for lunch. Then, everyone went their separate ways, except me. I tagged along with my brother, Mike. There was a reason. Mike had been on a roll, and he seemed to see deer every time he walked into the woods. I desperately wanted to share some of his action.

It didn't take us long to realize that the sudden onset of winter weather had pushed the rut into high gear. Everywhere, huge, hoof-dragging tracks crisscrossed the snow. We also noticed several scrapes had been reopened since the snow had stopped. Further, after being in the woods just 15 minutes, we jumped some deer. For lack of a better plan, we began trailing the five whitetails.

We had trailed the deer about 10 minutes when Mike suddenly stopped and whispered, "I know where these deer are going, Greg. They're headed for the big swamp."

I was familiar with the area. The big swamp was a huge expanse of low ground pretty much in the center of the hunting area. Stands of thick tamarack, impenetrable tag alders and head-high grass — and in wet years, knee-deep water — made the swamp a whitetail sanctuary. Every member of our group had experienced an ordeal with the big swamp.

Mike's initial assessment proved dead-on, because the deer headed for the swamp. I thought our trailing job was finished, but my brother had other plans. Instead of abandoning the trail, he plunged into the thick jungle. Of course, I had to follow.

We had followed the trail about 200 yards into the swamp when things went sour. The deer had slowed to a walk, and then split up and started meandering. Ten minutes later, we lost their trail among the tracks of numerous other deer that had cruised through the swamp earlier.

"We'll never catch up to those deer now," Mike said. "We might as well head out of here."

Soon, it became apparent that Mike didn't intend to follow our tracks out of the swamp. I voiced concern, but Mike said not to worry. He knew where he was.

"There's an oak ridge over that way a couple of hundred yards," he said, pointing straight ahead. "Paul is supposed to be over there somewhere. Maybe we'll push some deer his way."

As we later discovered, that's what happened.

Paul Connects on a Big Buck

Like all of us, Paul knew a couple of spots where we could usually see deer, including the oak ridge where Mike and I were heading. However, we didn't know that Paul hadn't reached his ambush spot when deer began boiling out of the swamp. Several antlerless deer passed him out of range, and then there was a lull. Paul slowly moved closer to the ridgetop. He was still about 15 yards from his stand when he saw a flash of gray on the ridgetop 50 yards away. Then, he saw the unmistakable glint of antlers. A big buck was trotting toward him!

Paul immediately stepped behind a tree and nocked an arrow. The monster deer quickly closed within 25 yards. After stopping briefly to scan his surroundings, the buck continued. Paul raised his bow and pointed the arrow at a small clearing on the ridge above. Soon, the buck was standing in the clearing 15 yards away. Paul came to full draw with his 50-pound Pearson bow and let it fly. There was a loud "crack," and the buck bounded away along the ridgetop.

Paul was heartsick. He was certain he had blown a point-blank shot at one of the biggest bucks he'd ever seen. Judging by the loud crack, Paul assumed his arrow had struck a tree. He walked to the ridgetop to look for the arrow, which he found immediately.

Soon, the buck was standing in the clearing 15 yards away. Paul came to full draw with his 50-pound Pearson bow and let it fly.

The buck had let us walk to within a few yards before jumping from his bed.

However, it wasn't stuck in a tree. The shaft was atop the snow next to lots of deer hair.

Paul followed the buck's tracks. He had traveled only a short distance when he found some small specks of blood. Then, he found more specks. He followed the fleeing deer's tracks farther and found a much heavier blood trail. Then, Paul knew it was time to gather the troops and form a plan.

Mike and I were the first to hear Paul's shouts. We walked to him, and he excitedly showed us the blood trail. We decided to build a small fire and wait for the rest of the group. It wasn't long before Richie, Bill and Rabs arrived, and we gathered around the fire. Between sips of hot chocolate and mouthfuls of sandwiches, we devised a plan.

None of us had been in this situation before. Thankfully, however, we made the right decision. The two most respected members of our group, Bill and Mike, decided we should push the buck, at least initially.

"It's obvious that Paul's arrow didn't hit the buck through the lungs," Mike said. "He's bleeding pretty good. We shouldn't have any problem following him in the fresh snow. A few of us should stay on his trail, and a few of us should circle ahead. Hopefully, somebody will get a shot at him."

Paul, Mike and I stayed on the buck's trail, and Bill, Richie and Rabs tried to intercept the buck somewhere ahead.

We didn't know we were about to start an almost six-mile chase, or how many close calls we'd have with the big buck before the day ended.

On the Trail

The buck ran almost a mile before showing signs of slowing. Then, it walked across a back-country road and headed into a small woodlot. We gave Bill, Richie and Rabs some time to take stands around the woodlot before continuing on the trail. Paul, Mike and I were almost at the end of the woodlot when a sudden explosion of snow, brush and gray hair erupted in front of us. The buck had let us close within a few yards before jumping from his bed.

Paul, Mike and I raced to the edge of the woods and immediately saw the buck. The big deer was 100 yards away, running among a herd of sheep across a large, open pasture. We watched the buck closely until it reached some timber on the far side of the pasture. We noted where the buck entered the woods. That saved us from having to track the deer through the sheep tracks, which would have cost valuable minutes.

Like before, we gave the three standers time to get ahead of the buck. At a prearranged time, Paul, Mike and I again started trailing the deer. Instead of continuing on a straight line, as we had anticipated, the buck suddenly took a hard left, squirted out of the timber and crossed another road.

As Paul, Mike and I exited the timber, we noticed a rural mail-carrier's vehicle in the road.

"That's one heck of a buck you guys are chasing," the mailman said excitedly. "He jumped out onto the road right in front of my car. He ran across this field and went into that little patch of woods. I've been watching, but I haven't seen him come out yet."

With that, the mailman wished us luck and drove away.

A Close Call

It took almost 30 minutes to round up Bill, Richie and Rabs. During that time, we closely watched the small patch of woods. Nothing stirred. I vividly remember thinking we had the buck that time.

Instead of using three trackers and three standers, we decided that only Mike and I would stay on the buck's trail, and Paul would join the standers. We had the small woods surrounded. Someone would surely get a shot — or so we thought.

As Mike and I neared the woods, we noticed the buck had jumped a tight, four-strand barbwire fence along the field edge.

"He can't be hurt very badly if he can still jump a fence like that," Mike said.

I had just put my hand on the top strand and was about to reply when the ground erupted on the other side. The buck had cleared the fence but had piled up soon afterward. He didn't jump until I put my hand on the fence.

If you've never experienced it, a mature buck six feet away appears gigantic. That's especially true if you're a rather small 14-year-old. Even Mike, who was considerably larger, was shaken. Several minutes passed before we could say anything.

"He's heading for the west side of the woods," Mike finally said. "Richie and Bill are over there. One of them will get a shot at the buck for sure this time."

Because of what we found and the way the buck stumbled when he ran, we were convinced the chase was almost finished.

We crossed the fence and studied the ground where the buck had fallen. What we found and the way the buck had stumbled when he ran convinced us the chase was almost finished — especially if Richie or Bill could shoot the deer again.

Mike and I waited until Paul joined us before again trailing the buck. We expected to hear excited talking as we neared the western end of the woods, but we didn't. In fact, we heard no talking. Surprisingly, Richie and Bill weren't there when we walked out. We learned later they had stood just beyond where the buck left the woods.

We Finally Catch Up
Paul, Mike and I figured our best option was to press on. The buck

Our group could think of no better way to end archery season than fresh tracking snow and rutting bucks.

had run into another small woods, and it became apparent he was weakening. We had walked less than 100 yards when we found a bed. Then, we found another and another. We were studying the third bed when we heard the buck in thick brush ahead. Immediately, we resumed trailing the deer. The buck crossed another road, but we were right behind him.

The final showdown occurred in the middle of a large cranberry bog. The hog-bodied 8-pointer could run no more. After some tricky maneuvering over the frozen bogs, Mike slipped within range of the big whitetail. However, the wear and tear of the chase and the excitement of the moment had also caught up with us. Mike's first two arrows were clean misses. He then caught his breath and collected his nerves. The third arrow found its mark.

Of course, Bucky didn't believe us when we called and said we had killed a big buck. I'm sure he became suspicious when we said he could pick us up at the farmer's place four miles from where he had dropped us off that morning. I'll never forget the look on his face when he pulled into the farmer's yard and saw us standing over the deer. The 8-pointer had an inside spread of 19½ inches and field-dressed at just less than 200 pounds.

A Valuable Lesson Learned

We didn't know it, but we had made the right decision about trailing Paul's buck. As we discovered at the end, Paul's initial shot hit the buck in the knee joint of the right front leg. Unbelievably, Paul's 50-pound bow had flung the cedar arrow and Bear Razorhead with enough force to break the buck's leg and sever an artery. By staying on the buck's trail, we ensured that it wouldn't have time to bed and staunch the blood flow. It's a lesson I've never forgotten.

The 8-pointer was one of the first big bow-kills in that area. Further, the hunt and ensuing trailing job lit a fire in my soul that still burns brightly.

My First Big One

During the past 14 years, I've written three books and hundreds of magazine articles about hunting whitetails. Regardless of the themes for those books and articles, one thing has remained: I try to include lots of anecdotes about my hunts. As one editor once said, anecdotes help break up the monotony of what might otherwise be a boring article. Actually, the editor's words were more like, "Anecdotes help just about any article flow more smoothly."

So after 14 years, three books and hundreds of articles, you might think I've long since written something about all my hunts. That's not true. More unbelievably, I've never written about the first huge buck I killed.

Perhaps that's because my success had little to do with deer hunting abilities. I was just in the right place at the right time.

The Story Unfolds

The story began during a Saturday morning in early November 1968. Three buddies and I were bow-hunting some rugged, wooded bluff country about 10 miles from our home town. Our bow-hunting efforts seldom entailed waiting to ambush whitetails. Our favorite — and therefore most productive — strategy was "walk, stalk and shoot." That's what we did that day.

We had walked into the bluffs from different directions early that morning. Besides trying to spot and stalk deer, we hoped any whitetails we jumped would move past another hunter. As usual, the strategy worked, at least to some degree. I had seen several deer during the first couple of hours, including one dandy buck. However, nothing had wandered within bow range.

I eventually reached the top of a steep hogback ridge. A well-used runway ran down its middle. As I eased along the runway, I begin noticing fresh buck sign. The runway was lined with rubs. Some of the trees that had been rubbed were as large as my waist. I also saw several steaming scrapes.

Something clicked inside my head, and I slowed my pace.

I had walked about 100 yards when the ridgetop began to widen somewhat. I took several more steps to the edge of a small clearing, which was mostly covered with shin-high yellow grass. About a half-dozen stunted oaks and as many small spruce trees dotted the clearing. I was absorbing the beauty of the spot when I noticed a small spruce tree 15 yards to my left shaking violently. Moments later, I saw why. A large buck was grinding its antlers against the trunk!

I quickly grabbed an arrow from my quiver and nocked it. Just then, the buck walked out from behind the tree, stopped and looked away. I came to full draw with my Bear Kodiak recurve, took what I thought was careful aim and released. The arrow flew inches over the buck's back.

The errant shaft hit a tree on the other side of the buck with a loud crack. Still unaware of my presence, the buck whirled and charged toward me. It seemed everything suddenly went into slow motion. I'm sure the sequence lasted only seconds, but it seemed like hours. The monster 8-pointer ran past me at less than three feet.

Initially, I thought the buck had charged me. It wasn't until I sat — weakly — and analyzed the incident that I determined the truth. The buck had heard the arrow hit the tree behind him and had fled in the opposite direction. I was just standing near his flight path.

I doubt that monster 8-pointer ever saw me.

Gun Season Opens
Two weeks after my encounter with the big buck, Wisconsin's

nine-day gun-deer season opened. Rather than head for our deer camp in northern Wisconsin, my dad decided we'd be better off hunting near home. The Northern deer herd had been decimated by consecutive severe winters, but there was no shortage of white-tails in the Chippewa County farmland we planned to hunt. In fact, much of the county was open to either-sex hunting the first two days of the season. Interestingly, Dad decided we'd hunt the same bluffs where I had the close encounter with the big buck.

During opening morning of gun season, I used almost the same strategy I had while bow-hunting: alternately walking and sitting. It was an effective way to see deer, but wasn't as effective at providing a clear shot at a buck.

I finally realized that deer were much more nervous and flighty than they had been during bow season because of the sudden influx of hunters and periodic rifle volleys echoing through the valleys.

About midmorning, I finally decided to stop pushing deer to other hunters. I found a comfortable spot on a south-facing hillside and plopped my butt on the ground. I would stay put till lunch time.

Earlier that morning, my brother Mike and I had vowed that we would hold out for bucks. Dad had overheard our conversation and quickly pointed out that our No. 1 objective was to put venison in the freezer.

"I don't want you guys to hesitate if you see a mature doe," he said. "It would be nice if we could all shoot bucks, but remember, we can't eat the horns. Besides, does taste a lot better than bucks anyway."

The morning hunt had convinced me that I should heed Dad's advice. If a mature doe appeared and I had a good shot, I would take it. Three hours of horn-hunting had been enough. Besides, I was eager to try the new Remington Model 600 .308 I'd purchased during summer. Dad had helped me develop a special handload for the gun, and I was anxious to see how it would perform.

However, I couldn't have imagined what I was about to experience.

Dad decided we'd hunt the same bluffs where I'd had a close encounter with the big buck two weeks earlier.

A Second Chance

I stayed on the hillside until about 11:30 a.m. Obviously, most of the other hunters on the bluff had also quit moving. Deer activity and shooting had almost stopped. Dad, Mike and I had agreed to meet for lunch between noon and 1 p.m. I had a hike ahead, so I got up and began walking toward the vehicle.

Dad had parked the car at the farm of a family friend, and it took me about 15 minutes to get there. As was his habit, Dad had locked the doors and pocketed the keys. I stood around the vehicle for a while, looking in the windows at the bags of sandwiches and the thermos of hot chocolate. I waited until 12:15 p.m., but no one showed up. I had a choice. I could remain at the vehicle and stare at those sandwiches — and listen to my belly growl — until Dad arrived, or I could return to the woods and hunt for a half-hour or so. Thankfully, I chose the latter.

About 300 yards behind the farmer's barn, a narrow strip of timber jutted from the bluffs. I decided to walk through the timber and check the fields on the other side. More than anything, I hoped I'd find Dad somewhere. However, I also knew that most local hunters would be leaving the woods to eat lunch. Through the years, Dad had repeatedly said that midday is a great time to be on stand.

"Hunters sometimes spook deer when they're walking out of the woods to go eat lunch," he said. "It's possible that one of those spooked deer might end up coming past your stand."

The fields I was approaching were bordered on three sides by wooded bluffs. I knew that one of my classmates and his two brothers had stands in one of the bluffs. I also knew they always returned to their home farm for lunch. So, I decided to set up at a spot that provided a good view of the fields where they would walk.

I sat for about 20 minutes but didn't see or hear a thing: no deer, hunter activity or shooting. I started thinking I was too late — that the noon rush was probably finished. I looked around one last time and then turned to leave. I had only taken a couple of

Mike and I had vowed to hold out for bucks. However, Dad overheard our conversation and said we'd better not pass up a mature doe.

steps when I heard a large branch break on the bluff across the field. I turned and saw a huge buck running toward me.

At first, I thought my eyes were playing tricks on me. However, there was no mistaking the sight of that big buck. I dropped to one knee and found the deer in my scope.

I held no illusions. Yes, the buck was enormous, and yes, he was in the open. However, I'd never shot at a running animal. Further, the buck would be at least 150 yards away when he passed by. The farthest I'd shot at any animal was 30 yards. My skills would be put to the ultimate test.

Amazingly, I somehow calmed my nerves. Just before squeezing off the first shot, I recalled something Dad had told me. Like most fathers, he didn't encourage shooting at running deer. But thankfully, he'd provided me with practical advice in case the situation arose.

"You'll have to lead the animal a bit," he had said. "With the loads you're shooting, I'd suggest putting the cross-hairs right on the animal's nose. Follow it along, and then gently squeeze the trigger. Oh, and remember to keep swinging right on through the shot."

I waited until the buck was as close as he would get before touching off the first shot. It was a clean miss. I quickly chambered another round and shot again — another miss. Then, however, I realized why I was missing. I wasn't following through with my swing.

I centered the buck in the scope again, followed him for a few bounds and gently squeezed the trigger. I heard the telltale "whop" of a hit. The buck staggered slightly, made two more bounds and disappeared into the strip of timber through which I'd walked earlier.

I was more than slightly shaken, but I still marked where the buck had entered the woods. I took time to reload my gun before slowly moving to the spot. I immediately found a heavy, obvious blood trail.

It was decision time. Should I take up the trail immediately or try to get help from Dad and Mike?

I waited several minutes and then hollered, first for Dad and then for Mike. Neither answered. I waited several more minutes and hollered again. Still no answer. Then, I started thinking about some of the stories Dad had told me about losing deer to other "hunters." He said some people would tag a deer another hunter had shot and claim it as their own.

I wasn't about to let that happen.

Though I had little experience trailing wounded deer, I could see the buck was hit hard. After the deer entered the woods, he'd slowed to a walk. After 50 yards, though, the buck had resumed running. I saw where he had kicked up leaves and dirt as he bounded through the woods. I also saw that the buck was losing a lot of blood, so I expected I would walk up on him at any second.

The trail eventually led over a small ridge. I was standing at the bottom of the ridge, closely scrutinizing the opposite hillside, when I heard leaves rustle to my left. I turned my head and saw the buck getting to his feet just 30 yards away. I quickly fired a finishing round into the deer's shoulder.

I stayed put with my gun ready until the buck was still. It wasn't until I stood over the deer and admired his antlers that I suddenly realized it was the buck that had almost run me over two weeks earlier. There was no mistaking that light, wide 8-point rack or the buck's giant body, which weighed more than 230 pounds field-dressed. It was the same deer. How ironic.

For unknown reasons, we never took a photo of my first big buck. Of course, there was no way I could talk Dad into letting me get a head mount of my trophy. Still, all wasn't lost. Twelve years after shooting the 140-class 8-pointer, I secured a cape from a local taxidermist.

The buck's mounted head is proudly on display in my living room.

Valuable Lessons Learned

My first big buck taught me quite a bit. First, I learned that my archery skills in those days left much be desired. Being able to put

"Hunters sometimes spook deer as they walk out for lunch," Dad said. "One of those spooked deer might come past your stand."

I'd never shot at a running animal. Further, the buck would be at least 150 yards away when he passed by.

arrow after arrow into a pie plate at 20 yards didn't make me Mr. Automatic when shooting at a big whitetail 15 yards away. It took much more concentration and patience to kill deer than to punch holes in paper.

I also learned that if you do what you're supposed to, you can hit running deer at 150 yards. I'm thankful to my dad for his advice about shooting at moving animals and the many hours he spent with me at the target range. Although I carried a new rifle that day, I felt like the .308 was part of me. I had put dozens of rounds through the gun and had great confidence in it.

However, the most important lesson I learned was that I exploited a situation. It's one thing to have your dad or another veteran hunter tell you that deer activity sometimes increases at midday. However, it's another thing when a young hunter listens to such advice and applies it.

I still use that strategy today.

Dad and I Learn a Lesson

The snow started falling just after midnight. It had tapered to flurries when Dad and I put our guns and lunches in the truck just before daylight. Before getting in, we hesitated to look at the 4 inches of fresh snow that blanketed the ground.

"Isn't that beautiful?" Dad said.

"It sure is," I replied.

To deer hunters in our neck of the woods, there's nothing like fresh tracking snow.

It was the fifth day of Wisconsin's nine-day gun-deer season. Dad and I had been in the woods from daylight till dark the previous four days. We'd walked countless miles and sat motionless for untold hours. But so far, the bucks had eluded us. We knew our lack of success was because of the conditions. For four days, we had suffered through bluebird skies and cold temperatures. It had also been an extremely dry fall. A squirrel searching for acorns in the fallen leaves made almost as much noise as a stampeding herd of cattle. You couldn't move in the woods without every deer within a quarter-mile pinpointing your location.

But that day would be different. Dad and I sensed it. The previous four days had left us clueless about where bucks were hiding. No more. If the bucks in our hunting areas moved, we'd know it. Better yet, we could track those deer into their daytime hideouts and roust them.

Of course, that didn't guarantee success, but it pretty much guaranteed action. And after what we'd encountered the previous four days, that would be a major accomplishment.

The Hunt Begins

Unlike the first four days of the season, Dad and I decided we wouldn't hurry into the woods. Instead, we planned to cruise country roads west of our hometown for the first hour or so of daylight. We figured the fresh snow had likely made deer considerably more active, and we hoped to see a big buck feeding or cruising across open farmland. We'd watch the deer until it slipped into cover, and then flip a coin to see who would take up the trail and who would circle ahead and wait in ambush.

As the years pass, I've come to appreciate an element of those long-ago hunts: We never had to worry about trespassing. Our family had permission to hunt almost every chunk of property from the city limits of our home town to the banks of the Red Cedar River almost 15 miles west. We hadn't leased hunting rights, either. It was just a matter of knocking on doors and politely asking for permission. We'd also obtained permission to hunt lots of ground because my brother Mike and I had picked rocks, baled hay and done other summer chores for landowners.

How things change. The tens of thousands of acres I once had permission to hunt near my home town have slowly decreased to one several-hundred-acre farm. The only reason I can still hunt the place is because my cousin Mark owns it. I pray that the hard work and everyday struggles of dairy farming don't get the better of him.

But back to the story. If Dad and I saw a buck, we'd initiate Phase 2 of our plan. And if you've tracked a big buck after a fresh snow, you know the excitement and exhilaration that can provide. I'm sure you appreciate the anticipation Dad and I felt as we left town that morning.

Though our spirits were high, Dad and I hadn't forgotten reality. After all, it was the fifth day of the season. Local deer had been repeatedly poked, prodded, chased and maybe shot at the previous four days. Yes, the snowfall might make some big bucks temporarily throw caution to the wind. However, those deer would immediately revert to their secretive ways if they sensed the slightest danger. We had our work ahead of us.

As the years pass, I've come to appreciate an element of those long-ago hunts: We never had to worry about trespassing.

Dad and I had been on the road less than 15 minutes when we saw the first deer. Dense snow clouds had put daylight on hold, so we had to drive with our headlights on. We'd topped a slight rise in the road when the lights illuminated the eyeballs of a deer in the ditch about 75 yards ahead. Dad slowed the car, and we closed within 20 yards of the deer before it suddenly whirled and ran into the timber. We saw antlers at the same time. It was a big buck!

"Well, that didn't take long," Dad said. "Tell you what. It's still a bit early to take up his trail. Let's drive around for another hour or so, and then we'll come back and go after him. Sound OK to you?"

It sounded great. Though still somewhat of a greenhorn at tracking, I knew a bit about deer behavior. I figured the buck had probably only run a short distance and was likely seeking a place to bed for the day.

The next hour passed slowly. Try as I might, I couldn't stay focused. I kept thinking about the big buck. I was afraid someone would notice the fresh tracks in the ditch and pursue "our" deer. Dad must have sensed my uneasiness.

"I don't think we have to worry about someone else seeing the buck's tracks," he said. "We've been driving around for nearly an hour, and we've only seen two other vehicles with hunters. And we haven't seen a single hunter walking around anywhere. Looks like we'll have that buck all to ourselves when we go back."

I Get Schooled

After what seemed like eternity, Dad and I returned to where we'd seen the buck. I lost the coin flip, which meant I would trail the buck first. Dad told me where he planned to stand.

"That buck was trying to cross the road when we came along and spooked him," he said. "I'd be willing to bet that he'll make a circle and come right back and try to cross here again. I'm going to walk up in the woods a little ways and stand where I can see his tracks from earlier this morning."

I followed the buck's trail and walked at a good clip until I found where he had slowed to a walk. The deer had traveled in almost a straight line for about a quarter-mile. Then, he had meandered a bit, walking through several patches of thick brush. I knew the buck was seeking a place to bed, so I slowed considerably and began paying more attention to the ground ahead.

The buck's trail went over a steep ridge. About halfway down the opposite side, the trail took a sharp left turn. I saw his tracks in the snow 50 yards ahead, still heading west. That's when I made a mistake.

Instead of easing along, I picked up the pace. My eyes were riveted on the buck's tracks where they topped a slight rise. I reached the top of the rise and was studying the ground when I heard a deer busting through thick brush to my right and slightly behind me. I caught a couple of fleeting glimpses of the deer as it bounded away.

I returned to the buck's trail, convinced that I had jumped a different deer. After 50 yards, however, I knew I'd blown it. The buck's trail suddenly veered right, went down the hillside about 20 yards and turned right again. From there, it led into the thick brush where I'd jumped the deer minutes earlier. I felt like a fool.

The buck had pulled a perfect button-hook. He'd let me walk 30 yards past where he had been bedded. Had I moved slowly and looked around instead of walking quickly and staring straight ahead, I probably would have killed him. Round 1 went to the buck.

There was still hope, though. As Dad predicted, the buck headed toward the road where we'd first seen him. Excited that Dad would likely even the score, I breezed along the buck's trail. It became apparent the buck was headed straight for Dad. I continued, expecting to hear a rifle shot any second, but it never happened.

I was a few hundred yards from Dad when I noticed the buck had suddenly made a hard left turn. Before that, he had been traveling in delicate 10-foot strides. After the turn, however, he had accelerated to 20- to 25-foot "I'm-out-of-here" bounds.

I soon learned why.

A group of hunters was walking single file atop the bluff above me. They hadn't seen the buck, but he'd sure seen them.

To say I was heartsick was an understatement. If the other hunters hadn't been there, the buck would have run to Dad. However, the buck had crossed the road about 200 yards north of Dad's setup. I followed the tracks to the road and whistled for Dad. He pulled up in the truck minutes later, and I explained the situation.

I could see disappointment on his face.

A Close Call

After crossing the road, the buck had angled across a picked corn-field and run into a small but extremely thick woods bordered by roads to the west and north. Dad suggested that we check the road to see if the buck had crossed out of the woods. Ten minutes later, we returned. The buck was still in the small woods.

Before again taking up the trail, we decided to have a sandwich and hot chocolate. We were about halfway finished with lunch when we noticed two pickups approaching. The trucks stopped near the edge of the small woods, and two hunters got out of each vehicle.

To our horror, the hunters started walking across the picked corn-field near the woods edge. They stopped one by one, taking up positions about 75 yards apart. Then, after a signal from the last hunter, the men walked into the woods to make a drive.

I rolled down my window to listen for shots. Dad watched the road ahead and the field where the drivers had walked into the woods. Maybe the buck would slip out the side or sneak back between the drivers. I held my breath and hoped the buck wouldn't make a mistake and run past a stander.

Twenty minutes later, we saw a pickup loaded with hunters pull up to the trucks parked ahead. The drive was obviously finished. We had-n't heard any shooting, but to satisfy our curiosity, Dad pulled ahead to ask whether the hunters had seen anything.

"There were some fresh tracks in the woods, but we didn't chase anything out," one of the hunters said. "Guess the deer must be hold-ing pretty tight today."

As we drove away, Dad looked at me and winked.

"That buck must have lain down and let the drivers walk right by him," he said. "We'll wait until those guys drive away, and then we'll go back and take his track. It'll be interesting to see what happened."

I was as curious as Dad and immediately volunteered to trail the

Dad drove within 20 yards before the deer whirled and ran into the timber. We saw antlers at the same time.

For hunters in our area, there's nothing like fresh tracking snow.

buck. I had to see how the deer had managed to escape.

Another Lesson

Ten minutes later, I was back on the buck's trail. Dad had debated where to stand, but eventually set up at a deer crossing along the north road. It seemed he had chosen correctly, because the buck's trail headed straight north.

I was about halfway through the woods when I found where the buck had lain. I also noticed something else. The buck had left the bed earlier. Instead of jumping and running, he had apparently crawled on his belly for some distance. Then, he had stopped in a patch of head-high blackberry briars. That's how he had eluded the drivers!

Since my first year at deer camp, I'd heard about big bucks supposedly crawling on their bellies to evade hunters. Until that November

1969 day, however, I was convinced those were just stories. I didn't think whitetails had the intelligence to pull off such a maneuver. I was wrong. The proof was in the snow at my feet. There was no doubt the buck I was trailing had crawled on his belly to escape detection.

However, there also was no doubt that I had jumped the buck from his bed in the briar patch. To my delight, he had again headed north. Unfortunately, the buck veered slightly east before reaching Dad. He had given us the slip again, but we were getting closer. We figured it was just a matter of time, and four hours of daylight remained.

Dad knew I needed a break, so he volunteered to track the buck into the next block of woods. The section was bordered on the east by a busy four-lane highway, so we quickly determined the buck wouldn't head that way. Further, a huge expanse of open ground bordered the woods to the north.

"There's always the possibility that the buck might make a circle and come right back across this road," Dad said. "But I'd be more inclined to believe he's going to head out the western side. That's a pretty big chunk of ground on the western side of the road, and I'm sure the buck knows that."

I waited until Dad disappeared into the woods before driving to the western side of the woods. I figured I had two options: a brushy fence line that ran from the woods to the road, or a narrow strip of tall, yellow grass and scattered clumps of tag alders. The strip of grass and brush also extended from the woods to the road — a natural buck crossing.

I jumped out of the truck, loaded my rifle and walked about 100 yards to the cover. I found a spot that provided a view of where the strip joined the woods, so I figured I could see the buck coming for about 200 yards. I backed into a clump of tag alders and began my vigil.

An hour passed. I was getting antsy and starting to second-guess my choice when I heard a sharp whistle behind me. I turned my head and saw Dad standing on the road. He motioned for me to join him. The sinking feeling in my stomach became more intense as I neared Dad. I suspected that I'd guessed incorrectly about where the buck would exit the woods.

I had.

I joined Dad at the truck, and he quickly filled me in.

"The buck kept heading northeast until he was within sight of the highway," he said. "Then, he bedded down. I jumped him from his bed but never saw him. From where he was, the buck could actually see the cars going by on the highway. But when I jumped him, he doubled-back and headed straight west. He came out of the woods right next to that brushy fence line just north of where you were standing. He followed the fence line all the way out to the road. That darn deer ran across 80 acres of open ground! He's in that big section to the west now."

A Final Lesson

Dad and I decided to continue after the buck. Although the section where the buck was hiding wasn't large, it didn't contain much cover. There were some grassy sloughs and brushy fence lines, and just enough deep valleys to let the buck remain unseen from the road. There was a 40-acre pine plantation in the northwest corner, and we figured that's where the buck had headed.

Dad resumed trailing the deer, and I drove to the pines. It was futile. As I learned later, the buck had already reached the plantation. He hadn't stopped running after crossing the road. However, as Dad subsequently told me, the deer shouldn't have made it.

Dad followed the tracks through a grassy slough when he saw a hunter ahead. The man was standing on a tall elm stump, looking away. The buck's trail led straight toward the guy. Dad first thought the buck must be in the grass between him and the hunter. However, as Dad approached, he saw where the buck had veered slightly and run past the hunter.

Dad was only 30 yards away before the guy turned and saw him.

"Been here long," Dad said.

"Since daylight," the guy replied. "I saw one small doe about 8:30. The deer just don't seem to be moving much today."

Dad sneaked a look at the buck's tracks.

"Yeah, it's kind of slow," he said. "Well, I'd better get moving. My son is waiting for me by that pine plantation up ahead. Good luck."

To this day, Dad and I chuckle about that. If the hunter had just

I jumped out of the truck, loaded my rifle and walked 100 yards into cover. From there, I could see where the strip joined the woods.

turned his head and looked to the left, he would have seen the buck coming from 200 yards away. As it was, the deer ran within 30 yards of the guy, saw him and then ran across 200 more yards of open ground. Unbelievable!

As I mentioned, the buck had beaten me to the pine plantation. Dad arrived a half-hour later, and we discussed our plan.

"We only have about an hour of hunting time left," Dad said. "I'll take the track into the pines and see if I can roust the buck out of there. My guess is that he'll make a circle and come right back out this side. You might as well stay right here."

I set up about halfway along the east side of the pines. About 15 minutes after Dad disappeared, I heard brush breaking to my right. Then, Dad appeared at the edge of the pines.

"The buck made a small circle and was going to come out right

Dad and I have often talked about who learned more that day: us or the deer. I often wonder what happened to that buck.

here," he said. "But his tracks turn and go back into the pines. He must have seen you."

Obviously, I had been looking to my left. Amazingly, the buck hadn't made a sound.

The story pretty much ends there. Dad stayed on the buck's trail for another half-hour, but the deer continued to circle in the pines. He was safe as long as he stayed in the pines — and he knew it.

What We Learned

Perhaps the most interesting thing we learned that day was that big bucks will run with the wind at their tails. After that buck realized something was trailing him, he traveled with the wind at every opportunity, obviously wanting to smell the threat behind him and trusting his eyes to see danger ahead. That's doubtless why he didn't hesitate to travel across open ground. In fact, his vision saved him from the hunter on the stump. The buck had seen the guy and detoured around him.

I also learned that big bucks will crawl on their bellies to evade hunters and possibly other predators. In addition, I learned that you must always pay attention when trailing deer. Had I been looking around instead of staring ahead, I could likely have shot the buck during the first hour of the hunt.

Dad and I have often talked about who received more education that day: us or the deer. Judging by the buck's body and antlers, I'd say he was 3½ at the oldest. However, that episode doubtless increased the buck's intelligence and cunning to that of a much older whitetail. I often wonder what happened to the buck.

Oh, I learned another important lesson that November day: You don't have to kill a deer to have a memorable hunt.

My Last Buck?

I was sitting at my work station at Elmendorf Air Force Base in Anchorage, Alaska, when I received the orders. My duty flight officer walked by and dropped some papers on my desk.

"Congratulations," he said sarcastically. "You're being reassigned to a place called Da Nang."

My heart skipped a beat. I was going to Vietnam!

It was early October 1972. I'd been in Alaska for almost 18 months, which had passed amazingly fast. For a young man with a strong passion for the outdoors, Alaska was paradise, featuring salmon fishing in spring and summer, big-game hunting in fall and rabbit hunting during winter. I'd never seen a place — and still haven't — with so many photographic possibilities. It was an incredible, memorable experience.

However, the orders called for me to leave Alaska in January. I'd receive three months of flight schooling and survival training in the states. I was also scheduled for two weeks in the Phillipines, where I'd take a course in jungle survival. From there, I'd travel to Da Nang in South Vietnam. According to the assignment sheet I'd received with my orders, I would be a member of an "airborne advance intelligence gathering squadron." In English, that means I would be a crew member aboard an EC-47 airplane. Our job was to search for and pinpoint "hot" targets. If we succeeded, we got out of the way and let armed aircraft do their thing.

And contrary to the terminology of the day, it was a war — not a conflict.

But Home First

The first thing I did after receiving my orders was to apply for a 30-day leave. I wanted to go home to Wisconsin and be with my family for a while. However, I decided to delay my leave for a month so I could see my family and hunt in Wisconsin's nine-day gun-deer season. I couldn't think of a better going-away present.

My mom and dad were very happy when I called to tell them I was coming home for a month. However, I received stunned silence when I told them about my orders for Vietnam. Dad was especially angry.

"I don't want you going over to that damn war," he shouted. "I don't see how they can send you from Alaska to South Vietnam. It just doesn't make any sense."

I agreed, but reminded Dad that orders were orders.

"It could be worse," I said. "If I hadn't enlisted in the Air Force, I probably would have been drafted into the Army. I'd most likely be in the infantry and fighting on the ground right now. I'd rather take my chances in the air."

I told Dad about my plans to be home for deer season.

"I've missed the past two seasons, and I'm anxious to come back and spend some time in the woods," I said. "I'd like to hunt around home for a few days and then head up North to the cabin."

Dad said that suited him, and that he'd make sure to take vacation for the entire season. He also said he'd contact my brother Mike and let him know I was coming home.

Surprisingly, I thought little about the war during the long plane ride home from Alaska. I was more concerned with seeing my family and visiting friends. And of course, I thought about whitetails. I'd return to Wisconsin in time to catch the last week of the early archery season. Then, I'd have a week to prepare for gun season.

Hopefully, I'd cross paths with a big buck at some point.

A Bow-Hunt with Friends

I spent the first of couple days resting and socializing with family and relatives. But by the third day, I had an incredible itch

Alaska was paradise for a young man with a strong outdoors passion. The time I spent there was incredible and memorable.

to hit the woods. I dug out my old recurve and some arrows, shot a few practice rounds and then called one of my hunting partners. He said several local bow-hunters were heading up North the next morning — Saturday — and that I was welcome to join them. He didn't have to ask twice.

My buddy picked me up before daylight the next morning. Six of us packed into his old Chevy Bel-Air for the two-hour drive to our hunting spot. Another hunting partner also had his car jammed full of bow-hunters. We planned to spend the first couple of hours that morning still-hunting. Then, we'd get together and make some small, well-organized drives the rest of the day. My buddies had used that strategy fairly effectively the past few weeks, and they predicted we'd see almost as many bucks as antlerless deer. I was pumped.

The day was more exciting than I'd anticipated. We moved deer past standers during every drive and even chased out a couple of black bears. I was the only one of our 12-man group who didn't get a shot that day. However, I couldn't have cared less. I saw dozens of deer, including a couple of whopper bucks. Best, however, I spent a beautiful November day with some of my closest, dearest friends doing something I cherished: chasing whitetails with a bow and arrow.

My Last Buck?

I've always thought the week before gun season was almost as fun as the season. Buying licenses, getting groceries, reloading ammunition, sighting in guns, finding equipment, and digging out and sorting through hunting clothes — they're all part of the yearly ritual. You'd think a week would provide plenty of time, but I always seem to encounter a last-second rush, and that season was no different.

My sister, Barb, would hunt with us the first two days of the season. Barb was a good hunter and a crack shot. Two years earlier, she had downed a beautiful buck with one shot from Dad's custom Sako .243. If I hadn't paced off the shot, I doubt I would have believed it. The buck was 230 paces from Barb when she anchored it — shooting offhand, by the way.

We spent opening morning roaming some rugged wooded bluffs seven miles west of our home town. We all saw deer, none of which wore headgear. We regrouped around noon and decided to head back home for lunch. Mike and I were cruising past a large Conservation Reserve Program field when I noticed a dark object about 500 yards away. I told Mike to stop so I could look at it through his binoculars.

It took a while, but I finally identified the object as a deer. However, the animal was lying flat with its head nestled behind a thick clump of grass.

"It's a deer and a big one," I said. "But I can't tell if it's a buck or a doe. Its head is hidden behind a clump of grass."

Mike told me to keep watching. He rapidly honked the horn on his Jeep twice. The deer never moved. Then, he rolled down his window and issued a loud, shrill whistle. The deer still didn't move.

We planned to spend the first two hours still-hunting, and then regroup and make small, organized drives.

"You know, I think I can sneak up on that deer," I said. "See that brushy fence line that borders the western side of the CRP? I can use that for cover until I'm in line with the deer. Then, I'll crawl through the fence line and use that little rise in the CRP field to stay hidden. When I pop over the rise I'll only be about 30 yards from the deer. If it's a buck, I should have time to get off at least a couple of shots before he makes it into the woods."

Mike agreed. He turned his vehicle around and pulled into a field road that was parallel to the brushy fence line. We were hidden from the deer by a small hill in the field.

"I can drive a little closer and save you some steps," Mike said. "Then, I'll go back out to the road and watch."

Our plan seemed foolproof. However, something unexpected happened.

I was about to leave Mike's Jeep when we saw a vehicle headed toward us on the field road. Another group had finished its morning hunt and was heading out. The hunters pulled alongside us, and the driver rolled down his window and hollered, "You guys seeing anything?" In a low voice, Mike said the morn-

The deer was gone.
Obviously, he had heard the
man talking, become nervous
and walked into the woods.

ing had been pretty slow. The guy then told us — loudly — about his morning. We could do nothing but sit and listen — and cringe.

The guy finally finished his story, wished us luck and drove away.

"It'll be a miracle if that deer is still there," I said. "But I'm going to make the stalk anyway."

The deer was gone. He had obviously heard the man talking, become nervous and walked into some nearby woods. Notice that I said "he." That's because I have no doubt the bedded deer was a buck — and a big one. The deer's bed was huge.

Mike and I drove home, grabbed a quick bite and resumed hunting. We spent the rest of the day still-hunting some bluffs. We saw several antlerless deer, but like that morning, neither of us saw a buck.

We returned home that evening and had a quick powwow with Dad and Barb. Dad suggested that instead of separating the next morning, we should push a small, isolated patch of brush he'd noticed early that day.

"It's just the kind of spot where a big buck would go to get away from all the pressure," he said. "It'll only take a few minutes to make the push, and then we can head for the bluffs."

Mike and I would make the push, and Dad and Barb would be the standers. Honestly, I wasn't optimistic. The small patch of brush was just that — small. It might have been five acres at the most. However, it was thick. A small tree surrounded by clumps of hazelnut brush and waist-high yellow grass stood at the center of the patch. It would only take minutes to push the area.

I had only walked about 20 yards into the patch when I started seeing deer sign. Runways and droppings were everywhere. Farther into the brush, I found a clump of fresh rubs. Mike was 50 yards to my left, and I heard him exclaiming about the sign he was finding. Still, I didn't hold much hope that we'd jump a buck.

Imagine my surprise when a buck suddenly sprang from its

I didn't have much hope that we'd jump a deer from the brush. Imagine my surprise when a buck sprang from its bed 15 yards away.

Just before leaving for Vietnam, I shot this 8-pointer. I wondered if it would be my last buck.

bed 15 yards away.

It was immediately apparent that the deer wouldn't cooperate with our plans. Instead of heading toward Dad and Barb, the buck cut between Mike and me and quickly disappeared in thick brush. I turned and sprinted back from where I had come. I ran as hard as I could for about 50 yards and then stopped. I brought up my rifle just as the buck disappeared behind a clump of brush, and then swung the gun to the far side of the brush as the buck reappeared.

Mike was still behind me and to my right, so I knew I had a safe field of fire.

I also knew I'd only get one shot. I swung the cross-hairs slightly ahead of the buck's nose and touched the trigger. At the recoil, I momentarily lost sight of the deer. However, I heard Mike yell, "You got him! Nice shot!" Then, I saw the buck lying on the ground.

That's not the end of the story. Mike and I reached the downed

This photo was taken during one of my airborne combat missions in Southeast Asia.

buck at the same time. We thought it was odd that the deer wasn't kicking or making death struggles. In fact, the buck's eyes had rolled back in his head, and he was stiff. Further, there was no blood.

"Where the heck did you hit him?" Mike said.

"I don't know," I replied. "I just swung the cross-hairs ahead of him and squeezed off a shot. From the way he piled up, I thought maybe I hit him in the neck."

Mike walked to where the buck had first plowed into the ground. Then, he bent and picked something up. He turned around with an incredulous look on his face.

"Look at this," he said. "You shot his darned horn off!"

I quickly glanced at the piece of antler Mike held and then looked back at the buck. The deer's eyes were rolling back in place, and his body was losing that rigor mortis appearance. I immediately killed the buck with a neck shot.

That's the thing about deer hunting — you never know what will happen.

Conclusion

I learned an important lesson that November 1972 day. Big bucks seek refuge in small patches of cover. That knowledge has served me well during the years since I shot that 8-pointer.

My tour of duty in Vietnam passed unbelievably quickly. I was sent back to Kelly Air Force Base in San Antonio, Texas, after it ended. I was discharged from the service four months later. I couldn't wait to get home, because my exposure to war had provided new perspective about the value of family and friends.

Also, it made me realize how much I cherished the privilege of chasing whitetails.

A Big Buck on Purpose

I'm often asked if I can single out a hunt that prompted me to become a serious trophy hunter. Actually, I remember the exact day and time when my approach to deer hunting changed forever. It was the first time I killed a big buck on purpose.

It's not that I hadn't killed any big bucks before that day in 1976. I'd killed a couple of dandies, including the one chronicled in Chapter 2. However, I don't consider that big 8-pointer an "on-purpose" kill. Although I knew about the buck, I hadn't hung my hat for the deer. It was just a matter of being in the right place at the right time. The only skill I displayed involved shooting.

That wasn't true with the big buck I killed in 1976. I knew about the deer and had hunted him the final three weeks of the early archery season. I saw the stout-bodied 8-pointer often during that three-week span. However, I couldn't get him within bow range.

Eventually, I figured out the deer's pattern. But more on that later.

How it Started

The hunt occurred in a large block of timber in northwestern Wisconsin. I'd spent the previous two years and much of the 1976 archery season trying to become familiar with the area. Earlier that year, loggers had clear-cut a 120-acre section from the southeastern corner of the block. By fall, the logged area was rich with grasses, weeds and young poplar shoots. Also, it held abundant discarded treetops. The spot had become a deer grocery store.

My hunting partners and I had closely watched the clear-cut

throughout the early weeks of archery season. We saw deer activity in and around the area at all times. However, although we saw some small bucks early in fall, the big boys had maintained a low profile. Still, we were confident things would change as the rut approached.

Honestly, any guy in our group would have been tickled to arrow any buck. Back then, we had few archery kills under our belts. As with most bow-hunters of that era, we considered any bow-killed buck a trophy, regardless of its rack.

For that reason, I concentrated all my attention on the clear-cut. We'd been seeing bucks in the area since opening weekend, and I didn't care that most of them were spikes, forkhorns and 6-pointers. All that mattered was that they had antlers. I desperately wanted to ambush a buck by executing a well-conceived game plan.

I should reiterate an important point. That hunt occurred almost 25 years ago, before the current trophy whitetail craze. There were no specialty deer magazines. The few whitetail books available contained as much misinformation as practical knowledge. Therefore, most hunters used a trial-and-error approach. If a strategy worked, we stuck with it. If it didn't, we abandoned it.

And then there was our equipment. Yes, we had compound bows and aluminum arrows. However, those compound bows were only slightly better than recurves. We had no odor-killing detergents, odor-killing sprays, commercially manufactured cover scents or charcoal/carbon odor-filtration clothing, and few reliable deer scents or lures. We had tree stands — homemade, of course.

Those homemade stands were probably my most important piece of equipment. One of the first things I learned was that deer seldom — if ever — looked up. The few deer that looked up didn't seem to realize that an unusual blob in a tree might be a predator. Unbelievably, we rarely placed tree stands more than 10 feet high. There was no reason to go higher.

Hunting from a tree stand let me do something that I'd always dreamed about: closely observe whitetails. I can't tell you how much I learned those first few years. Doubtless, the most important lessons involved the feeding habits of big-woods deer. Like many hunters, I

Earlier in the year, loggers had clearcut a 120-acre section from the southeastern corner of the block. By the time hunting season rolled around, the spot had turned into a deer magnet.

was familiar with basic deer foods, such as acorns, grasses and poplar shoots. However, I didn't know whitetails also ate mushrooms, blackberry plants, poison ivy, freshly fallen maple leaves and various forms of browse.

I also learned something else. Just like their farmland relatives, big-woods deer could be patterned. More important, I discovered that antlerless deer patterns were almost always different than those of bucks.

That tidbit eventually let me kill a big buck "on purpose."

The Stage is Set

In Fall 1976, I was anxious to put my newfound knowledge to use. With bow in hand and a homemade tree stand slung over my shoulder, I headed into a chunk of timber that bordered one side of the clear-cut. It was late afternoon during a beautiful mid-October day.

I was less than 60 yards
from my stand when I saw a
set of huge, fresh tracks.
The buck had walked
through the area just before
I'd reached my stand.

There was a slight nip in the air, and the bucks were feeling frisky. I noticed several fresh rubs and a couple of new scrapes while walking to my spot.

My stand site was atop a timbered ridge that extended into the clear-cut. I'd scouted the area the previous weekend and found several deer were walking the ridgetop when traveling to and from the clear-cut. From what I determined, the deer were bedding in thick tag alders that bordered a small creek west of my stand. The area was fairly secluded, which gave me confidence that deer would move before dark.

The sun was hanging above the horizon when I heard a deer approaching from the creek bottom. Seconds later, I saw a 6-point buck walking on the ridgetop — straight toward me. I immediately grabbed my bow and got into position for what I thought would be an easy shot. However, in typical buck fashion, the 6-pointer did something unpredictable. Instead of staying on the runway, which passed 10 yards from my stand, he veered off the main trail and walked parallel to the ridgetop. Still, if he stayed on course, he'd pass within range.

I waited until the buck was in front of me before drawing my bow. The 6-pointer stopped to sniff the ground, and I released an arrow. The shaft flew just over the deer's back! Instead of running off, however, the buck took two delicate bounds before stopping to look around. I nocked another arrow and took careful aim. Unfortunately, I was so locked in on the buck's vitals that I didn't see a twig that stuck out in front of my target. I fired, heard a slight "ting" and saw my arrow veering off. The 6-pointer didn't stick around to provide a third try.

I knew why I'd missed the first shot. It had become a familiar pattern. Before that season, I'd mostly hunted from the ground. I had become pretty good at judging distances to animals on the same level. However, I was having trouble adjusting to judging distances to deer below. Even deer that were close looked smaller when I was perched on a tree stand, so I tended to overestimate the distance — and overshoot the deer.

I missed more than my share of point-blank shots the first couple of years I bow-hunted from a tree stand. Still, I had a ball. There was something magical about having whitetails walk by without knowing a predator was standing over their heads. If wind conditions were favorable and I didn't move too much, I never had to worry about getting picked off — never! That's amazing considering we almost never hung stands higher than 10 feet.

I was upset about missing two easy shots at the 6-pointer, but I stayed on stand until shooting hours ended. During the last 15 minutes, 15 whitetails left the creek bottom and traveled to the clear-cut. The last deer sported a large set of antlers.

As I soon learned, it wouldn't be the last time I'd see that buck.

The Rut Kicks Into Gear

Late October arrived quickly, as did an increase of buck activity. A hunting buddy and I were driving to our cabin one morning when we passed the clear-cut. We saw the big buck instantly. The hog-bodied deer was 200 yards out in the cut, tending a hot doe. He didn't even glance at us when we stopped.

We watched the buck nose the doe for a few minutes before it dawned on me: The buck was so absorbed with the doe that I could probably stalk close enough for a shot. I had my buddy drive up the road about 100 yards, hiding us behind a hill. I grabbed my bow and walked along the back side of the hill. I could hear the buck's loud tending grunts, and I used them to monitor his whereabouts. After 10 minutes of walking, I was in line with the deer. I nocked an arrow and eased to the hilltop.

I peeked over the top and immediately saw the buck's antlers. Then, I saw the back of his head. I couldn't believe my good fortune — the big deer was 20 yards away and looking in the other direction. I drew the bow and stood. That's when I saw the doe, standing alert and looking right at me. We immediately made eye contact.

The doe snorted loudly and took off like she'd been poked with a needle. The buck also bolted and stayed hot on the doe's tail for a while. Then, however, he split off and headed into a nearby finger of timber.

I saw the doe, standing alert and looking right at me. The doe snorted loudly and took off like she'd been poked with a needle.

This big-woods buck was the first whitetail I killed "on purpose." The hunt changed how I viewed the sport.

As I turned to walk to the road, I smiled. The big 8-pointer was in the same timber where I'd seen him during that earlier hunt.

I saw the big buck once more before the early archery season ended, just after daylight on a snowy November morning. I was late reaching my stand that morning, and the buck crossed the road in front of my truck. That time, however, he was coming out of the clear-cut. Although I knew the big buck wasn't in the immediate area, I hunted from my ridgetop stand anyway. I didn't see a deer, but I discovered something interesting on my trek out. Rather than taking my usual route, I swung to the edge of the clear-cut. I was less than 60 yards from my stand when I found a set of fresh, huge deer tracks, which had apparently been made just before I'd reached my stand.

My curiosity piqued, so I followed the tracks. As I suspected, they soon started angling south. Judging by their slight meandering pattern, the tracks had been made by a big buck cruising for hot does. Several minutes later, I reached the road. The big buck I'd been tracking was the one I'd seen cross the road that morning. Then, I realized the big 8-pointer had traveled through that finger of timber on the back side of the clear-cut three times.

Back on the Ridge Stand

I avoided the ridge until opening morning of gun season. I'd already developed a game plan for ambushing the big buck. Rather than sit in my tree stand site atop the ridge, I would move farther east and sit about one-third down the south side of the ridge. From there, I could see the edge of the clear-cut. More important, I could easily cover the timber where the big buck apparently walked when he cruised through the area.

Opening morning of the 1976 gun-deer season dawned clear, cold and calm. Snow from the previous weekend had melted after a couple of days, so the woods were loud and crisp for the first few hours. That let me hear the first deer when it was still 200 yards away in the clear-cut. After a long, heart-pounding wait, I finally saw it. It was a lone doe.

She walked into the strip of timber below, stopped briefly and then began walking briskly toward the creek bottom. I checked my watch. It was 7:30 a.m.

"If there's a buck following that doe, he should be coming along in the next 15 minutes or so," I thought.

But it wasn't to be.

Fifteen minutes passed, and then 20. I didn't even hear a squirrel stirring. Eventually, I stopped paying so much attention to where the doe had appeared. Ten minutes later, though, I heard the unmistakable sounds of a deer approaching from the east. I immediately turned in that direction.

Something about the deer's walk was different than that of the doe. It was more steady and deliberate. Also, although the doe had made noise, this deer seemed to go out of its way to make its presence known. Then, a loud grunt pierced the early-morning stillness.

My wife, Geralyn, poses with the mount of my 8-pointer — the first whitetail I had patterned and killed.

My heartbeat, which was already racing, hit another gear. Somehow, I knew it was him. The buck I'd been chasing for three weeks was bearing down on my stand!

The buck grunted twice more while still in the clear-cut. I honed in on him and watched in awe as the rut-swollen deer suddenly strolled into the timber. The buck stopped for a second to look around before flicking his tail and, with another loud grunt, continued ahead. If he stayed on course, the deer would pass below me at 40 yards — a piece of cake for my .308.

And the shot was a piece of cake. The big deer hunched slightly at the hit, turned to head back from where he'd come from and then tipped over dead.

A three-week quest had ended in seconds.

What I Learned

It wasn't until I stood over the buck that it dawned on me: I had patterned and killed a mature buck. Sure, the deer had slipped past several times during bow season, but I hadn't given up. More important, I had eventually pinpointed an area where the buck felt safe. I had learned it was possible to pattern mature bucks in the big North Woods.

The buck also taught me another lesson, although it took a couple of years to sink in. As I mentioned, my partners and I were still greenhorns at trophy hunting. We didn't know much about the right and wrong ways to do things, including how often to hunt a stand before you burned out a spot. About the only thing we paid attention to was wind direction, and we even took chances with that.

Anyway, I have no doubt that I overhunted my ridgetop stand. It was apparent that the big buck had determined that a human — me — was routinely invading his domain. Further, the buck knew exactly where I was walking and sitting. Then, he adjusted his travel routine just enough to bypass that spot. However, the buck hadn't adjusted enough to put him out of rifle range.

Thank goodness.

The Squirrel Hill Buck

In the previous chapter, I detailed how I patterned and killed a mature buck. I also mentioned that as I stood over the deer, I felt a great sense of accomplishment.

However, I didn't mention the slight cocky attitude I developed afterward. I remember thinking that I had patterning figured out. It was just a matter of finding a big buck early in the season and sticking with that deer until you had his patterns down pat.

As you might imagine, it wasn't long till I was knocked off my high horse. Actually, I was humbled early the next archery season. I couldn't complete the first part of my patterning "equation" — locating a mature buck. Of course, it didn't help that my construction job limited my hunting time to weekends. Still, it was frustrating that I couldn't at least get a glimpse of a big deer.

Eventually, I had to admit that the events of the previous year were somewhat of a fluke. I had been darned lucky to see the big 8-pointer early in the archery season and kill it during gun season.

Finally, in 1980 ...
Not many people know that I've been infatuated with bow-hunting big black bears for years. In fact, it was bear hunting that eventually resulted in my second "on-purpose" big buck.

It was late August 1980, three weeks before Wisconsin's bear season. During a free morning, I trudged down an old logging trail with 5-gallon pails of bear bait in each hand. Suddenly, I saw a large, velvet-antlered whitetail 40 yards away drinking from a small mud puddle on the edge of the trail. I quietly set down the pails and knelt. The buck continued to drink for several more seconds but suddenly snapped up his head. He saw me immediately.

As is often the case with mature bucks, the deer didn't panic. He merely turned and walked into a thick patch of blackberry brush. Just that quickly, he was gone. I didn't see or hear him run; he simply vanished.

Incidentally, I saw that buck while heading toward the Squirrel Hill Bait. Therefore, I called the deer the Squirrel Hill Buck.

Several weeks later, during the bear-season opener, I saw the buck again. I was watching a bait station along the edge of some mature red oaks when the deer strolled into view, heading toward the oaks. I watched the buck for almost a half-hour as he gobbled acorns. Then, just as he'd done during our first encounter, the buck disappeared.

But by then, I'd seen enough to know where I'd place my stand for archery season the next weekend.

The Hunt Begins

The next Saturday afternoon, I was perched in a portable tree stand in a tall red oak 10 yards from where the big buck had twice walked the previous week. About an hour after I settled in, a doe and two fawns walked into view. The deer soon fed within range of my stand. Later, the doe snapped up her head and stared toward some thick brush near the edge of the oaks. I was surprised to see a half-dozen deer stride boldly out of the brush. Four were antlerless, and the other two were identical forkhorns.

Though I wasn't aware of it then, my restricted hunting time actually had worked in my favor. Judging from the behavior of the does and small bucks, my infrequent intrusions hadn't created problems. So, I hunted the area throughout October, and I continued to see does, fawns and immature bucks. The Squirrel Hill Buck hadn't yet appeared, though, and I began to doubt that he would.

Then, however, something erased those doubts. About the third weekend of October, I started finding fresh antler rubs near the oaks. Some were obviously the work of the small bucks I'd seen. However,

Not many people know that for years, I've been infatuated with bow-hunting black bears.

I saw the Squirrel Hill Buck several weeks later on the opening day of Wisconsin's bear season.

I also found several thigh-sized trees that had been savagely rubbed. I deduced that those rubs were the work of a much bigger buck. My confidence was restored that the big 8-pointer was still around.

Fresh rubs continued to appear near the oaks as October waned. Then, during a cold late-October morning, I finally saw the Squirrel Hill Buck again. The deer entered the oaks near where I'd found a cluster of fresh, huge rubs earlier. The buck nosed through the oaks and eventually disappeared in some thick poplars on the far side.

I waited several minutes before climbing down and walking to where the buck had exited the oaks. I immediately saw a couple of rubs on 4-inch-diameter poplars. Unfortunately, the significance of that didn't sink in. I merely shrugged my shoulders and silently prayed that the buck would walk within range the next time.

My next hunt in the oaks occurred the morning of Nov. 1. I had enough experience to know that was a magical date. Bucks would be feeling the first stirrings of the rut, but most does wouldn't be ready to play the breeding game. I knew that could frustrate even the biggest bucks, often prompting them to become more active during daylight.

I'd been on stand about 30 minutes when I heard a deer approaching the oaks. Its deliberate stride and a telltale grunt confirmed that it was a buck. Seconds later, I detected movement near the edge of the oaks — right where I'd found the huge rubs a week earlier! I trained my attention on the spot and saw the big buck walk into view.

Although it was encouraging to see the deer, I knew immediately he wouldn't come within range. In fact, it seemed the buck kept a safe distance from my stand. At first, I found that confusing. After all, I had twice watched the buck walk within spitting distance of that spot. Did he somehow know I was there, or was there another reason for his new routine?

As he had done the previous weekend, the buck slowly walked through the oaks with his nose to the ground. I watched as the big 8-pointer exited the oaks at the same spot as before.

That's when reality hit me. The monster deer was following a line of fresh antler rubs — rubs he had likely made — when he traveled to and from the oaks.

Exploiting the Newfound Strategy

I waited for more than an hour after the buck disappeared before climbing down and seeking a new stand site. It took only minutes to find a tree that would put me in range of where the buck had walked through the oaks. I positioned my stand and took several minutes to evaluate the situation. As I looked around, I suddenly realized my stand site was almost dead center between the two rubbed areas I'd found earlier.

A deep feeling in my gut told me something good would happen there.

The big buck hadn't seemed suspicious when I saw him that morning, so I decided to hunt the oaks again — from my new stand site — that afternoon. Other than many squirrels that constantly scurried around, the first three hours were uneventful. However, that changed dramatically the last few minutes of daylight.

Soon, I heard deer running through the woods, and saw a doe and fawn headed toward me. They didn't stop until they were right under me. The deer quickly turned their attention to their back trail. Seconds later, I heard another deer slowly shuffling along the trail. I somehow knew it was the big buck — and I was right.

The deer closed within 75 yards before stopping. He stared at he doe and fawn for a half-minute, and then lowered his head and thrashed a 4-inch-diameter poplar. I prayed that the buck would stop rubbing and again follow the doe and fawn.

However, it wasn't to be.

I waited until darkness before climbing down, and I could still hear the 8-pointer grinding on the poplar as I sneaked out.

Third Sighting a Charm

I returned to my stand in the oaks before daylight the next morning. Thirty minutes into my hunt, a forkhorn sauntered by at 15 yards. That was it for a couple of hours.

However, about 9 a.m., I heard another deer approaching. I saw movement on the far side of the oaks and concentrated my attention there. The next thing I knew, the buck of my dreams was trotting

It realized that the monster deer was following a line of fresh rubs as he traveled to and from the oaks.

toward me.

I took a bearing on the buck's travel path and quickly picked out an opening where I could shoot. I came to full draw just before the buck reached the opening. I'll never forget what happened next.

The buck suddenly stopped and looked into my eyes. Initially, that threw me. However, my sight pin was locked on the deer's vitals, and the arrow was on its way a split-second later.

The buck instantly hunched and whirled after hearing the bow. As a result, the arrow struck the deer farther back than I'd intended. Nausea instantly hit me as I watched the deer bound away.

I waited about 15 minutes before climbing down to investigate. My deflated feelings were quickly replaced by optimism when I walked to where I'd last seen the buck. I immediately found the start of a profuse blood trail. (I later learned my arrow had missed the abdominal cavity and struck a major artery.)

I followed the trail about 200 yards to a nearby logging trail. Then, I marked the spot and went to find help.

I returned an hour later with my brother Jeff and another hunting partner. We soon eased along the buck's trail. As we followed the blood, I began to notice some interesting things. First, it was obvious that the buck was heading into the heart of his core area. Second, every runway the big deer followed was heavily marked with fresh rubs.

Believe it or not, the hog-bodied whitetail made it almost a half-mile before dying. The buck had a fairly wide — 18$\frac{1}{2}$-inch inside spread — 8-point rack. And as we discovered a couple of hours later, the deer field-dressed at just less than 220 pounds. He was truly a trophy.

I was proud of my accomplishment. After all, the 8-pointer represented the first mature buck I hunted exclusively and then killed. More important, my obsessive pursuit of the buck piqued my curiosity about the obvious relationship between bucks and their rubs.

After that day, my approach to the deer hunting changed.

I was so intrigued by my findings that I returned to the buck's stomping grounds later that fall. I was surprised and excited by what

Thirty minutes into my hunt, a small buck sauntered by at 15 yards. That's all I saw for a couple of hours.

I learned. My scouting forays proved that the big buck strongly related to and repeatedly visited his rubs. And as I had suspected, his travel routes were clearly marked by lines of rubs.

To say that information substantially increased my rub knowledge is an understatement.

Substantiating my Findings

Like a scientist on the verge of a great discovery, I couldn't wait to test my rub theories on other big bucks. I got to do that the next year, during the 1981 archery season. I was scouting an unfamiliar tract of big-woods real estate when I stumbled across a hot feeding area. It was immediately apparent that more than a dozen antlerless deer fed at the area. And, judging from the fresh rubs and scrapes I found near the perimeter of the food, several bucks were also routinely visiting the area.

Few people know this big-woods buck first interested me in antler rubs and rub lines.

At first, the abundant buck sign was encouraging. However, that encouragement soon turned to discouragement. I knew my first hunt at the area would be my best chance to kill a big buck, but the amount of sign made it almost impossible to single out the best stand site.

Initially, I thought I'd have to resort to guesswork. However, I recalled my experience with the big buck the previous archery season. Could I find a rub line that headed toward the food source?

To make a long story short, that's what I did. A week later, I killed a beautiful 10-pointer as he walked along a rub line where I waited in ambush.

That's what I call substantiating a theory!

What I Learned

The big 8-pointer gave me a crash course in Rub Lines 101. The 10-pointer I killed the next year further fueled my desire to learn more about that aspect of whitetail behavior. My quest reached a fever pitch the next few years. I haven't kept track, but I know many mature bucks have died because of my findings.

My success eventually compelled me to share my discoveries about rubs and rub lines. In late 1986, I wrote an article on the subject. It appeared in Fall 1987 in a national hunting magazine. Judging by the subsequent response I've received, many deer hunters are interested in the subject.

Many seasons have passed since I hunted the Squirrel Hill Buck. However, my memories from that pursuit remain eerily vivid. Perhaps it's because the big 8-pointer was such a special trophy.

The buck taught me more about mature buck behavior than any whitetail before. And as a result of those lessons, I eventually made the jump from a construction worker to full-time outdoor writer.

As I said, the Squirrel Hill Buck was a special trophy.

A Special Thanksgiving

If there's a recurring theme in this book, it's that big bucks seldom come easy.

I recall few hunts in which I ambushed a big buck after expending minimal time and energy. Typically, my pursuits stretched weeks, months or even years.

In the previous two chapters, I've discussed bucks I killed "on purpose." That is, I knew about the deer, and then patterned and killed them. Incidentally, that was a rare accomplishment in those days. Most bow- and gun-hunters just hoped for a chance at any deer.

I'd like to say the buck featured in this chapter was an "on-purpose" deer, but it wasn't. Sure, I knew about the deer, and I hunted him specifically during the first few weeks of the 1983 bow season. However, I gave up on the buck later in the archery season. When we crossed paths again during gun season, it was just coincidence.

That doesn't mean the hunt isn't an interesting story, though.

I 'Find' the Buck

Anyone familiar with my hunting style knows I'm a big proponent of scouting. No other factor has played a larger role in my consistent success. That's why it's somewhat humbling to admit that I didn't discover the buck in this chapter after a long, exhausting scouting mission.

During late August 1983, I learned about the deer. My wife, Geralyn, and I were driving on Highway 35 toward our cabin in northwestern Wisconsin. We were three miles from the cabin when I glanced at one of the few alfalfa fields in that part of the state. For some reason, I automatically looked at a back corner of the field. A deer was standing in the corner, and I immediately saw large antlers.

But just that quickly, we zoomed past.

"I just have to get a better look at that deer," I said excitedly. "If his rack is as big as I think it is, he's a real ringer!"

I turned around a quarter-mile up the highway. Less than a minute later, I parked on the shoulder of the busy highway, grabbed my binoculars and focused on the deer. My initial assessment was correct. He was a ringer!

Though only an 8-pointer, the buck featured good tine length and an impressive inside spread. The element that really caught my attention, however, was how the buck's antlers sat atop his head. He had one of those high racks hunters talk about. Plus, he was still in velvet, which made him appear more awesome. Not wanting to attract attention to the spot, I only studied the buck for a minute before driving away. I'd watch the field the next few weekends.

As was my late-summer custom, I was keeping my bear baits supplied with goodies. In those days, an archery deer license entitled you to kill a bear, so bear hunting was an annual ritual, providing a ready excuse to head for the cabin every weekend. (Honestly, I've never needed an excuse. Geralyn is always eager to join me on trips to the North Woods.)

Our routine the next three weekends was identical. We'd get home from work Friday evening, pack the truck, head for our cabin and check the alfalfa field for the big buck. Amazingly, we saw him three consecutive Fridays. More amazingly, we also saw him three consecutive Saturdays. Talk about a predictable pattern.

Buck or Bear?

I decided to wait until the Sunday before opening weekend of archery season to prepare my stand near the alfalfa field. Although the land bordering the field was public, I obtained trespass rights to the field from the landowner. I wanted to make sure my bases were covered.

Now, I must ask for understanding. Remember, it was 1983, and although I had deciphered much about big bucks, I still had a lot to learn. I didn't know I would receive a painful lesson about the rights and

I didn't know I'd soon receive a painful lesson about the dos and don'ts of pre-season scouting and stand selection.

wrongs of pre-season scouting and stand selection.

I'd already chosen the tree where I'd place my stand the next weekend. During the previous three weeks, I'd seen the buck feeding within range of a red pine. The Sunday before the season, I used branches to climb the tree and check things out. I was happy to see that I wouldn't have to trim anything. I quickly confirmed where I'd place my stand and climbed down.

However, I then did something that, to any serious deer hunter nowadays, bordered on insanity. Instead of leaving the area, I walked around. Actually, I walked quite a bit. I traveled the entire field edge and explored several well-used runways that led to the alfalfa. When I finished, I had stumbled around the area for more than an hour. I hadn't yet learned how costly that could prove.

Opening day soon arrived — with a big dilemma. One of my bear baits was red hot. My bear hunting partner and I knew at least a half-dozen bears were working the bait, including a whopper. Should I hunt bears or whitetails? To my partner, the choice was obvious.

"You gotta sit on your bear bait," he said adamantly. "That big bear you've got coming in will easily be heavier than 400 pounds. You probably won't get a chance at a bear like that again in your lifetime. But you'll have chances to shoot lots of deer."

My partner didn't know how badly I'd been bitten by the whitetail bug. That's surely why he looked at me like I was crazy when I told him I'd hunt the big buck.

"I'll have that deer dead on the ground a half-hour before shooting hours expire," I said. "Then, I'll have the rest of the archery season to concentrate on killing that big bear."

Geralyn and I hadn't made it up North in time to check the buck the Friday before opening day. It was dark when we cruised past the alfalfa field, but I wasn't worried. The big deer hadn't varied his routine the past three weeks. I thought it was almost a done deal.

The next day, Geralyn dropped me off at the alfalfa field four hours before dark. I wanted to be ready long before the buck headed for the field. I was still a relative rookie at the trophy whitetail game, but I knew that first hunt would provide my best chance.

I focused on the spot and was stunned to see the big 8-pointer stroll boldly to the alfalfa.

We awoke to find more than 14 inches of snow on the ground. We had hoped for snow, but this was ridiculous! Conditions had gone from one extreme to something even worse.

Time ticked past agonizingly slow. Then, the sun finally reached the horizon, and I knew things would start happening. Just like I'd envisioned the past three weeks, I knew the buck would saunter down the runway 12 yards from my stand. I just had to keep my composure long enough to seal the deal.

I watched the evening shadows lengthen and eventually disappear. The buck was officially late. I started to panic when I noticed movement on the field edge 60 yards away. I focused on the spot and was stunned to see the big 8-pointer stroll boldly out to the alfalfa. Why had he come out there?

The buck had always appeared relaxed and unconcerned, but that was no longer true. It was obvious the deer was suspicious and nervous. He'd only snatch a few mouthfuls of alfalfa before snapping his head up and scanning his surroundings. Then, the buck almost turned inside out when a raven whisked just over his head. He bounded twice toward the woods before stopping to see what had happened. Two minutes passed before he finally dropped his head and resumed feeding.

When the buck had entered the field, I thought he might feed toward me. However, I realized that wouldn't happen. It was apparent the buck was avoiding the part of the field where my stand was. I could only sit and watch the deer through binoculars until darkness. Then, I pulled my stand from the tree and climbed down.

The buck added insult to injury by snorting loudly as I walked to the highway.

Like any good deer hunter, I closely watched the alfalfa field during the next month. Also, I periodically scouted the woods that bordered the field. However, I never saw the buck or any sign that indicated he was still in the area. It was like he had disappeared. In hindsight, I'm sure the buck was still hanging out nearby. But because I lacked sufficient knowledge, I expected to find a batch of big-buck sign — during a time when big deer don't leave much sign! I guess you live and learn.

So, I gave up on the buck and sought greener pastures. I'm not certain, but I think I ate my archery tag that year. To make matters worse, I didn't kill a bear, either.

The 1983 hunting season had been far from memorable.

A Depressing Start to Gun Season

When I thought things couldn't get worse, they did. I'd found a great stand site for the firearms opener, but I'd only been on stand a few minutes that day when I heard what I thought was distant thunder.

"Nah, that couldn't have been thunder — not at this time of year (the third week of November)," I thought.

But seconds later, I heard it again. That time, it really sounded like thunder. Then came the clincher. I looked to the west and saw a heart-stopping cloud-to-ground lightning strike.

I didn't need to mull the situation long. I knew the last place I wanted to be was 30 feet up in a large pine tree holding a lightning rod — my .270. I quickly gathered my gear and scurried down that pine like a squirrel trying to escape a hawk. I reached my truck just as the skies opened up.

The thunderstorm lasted most of the day, dumping almost 5 inches of rain in northwestern Wisconsin.

Because of the rain, the second day of the season was also a wash. During Day 3, the bottom dropped out of the thermometer. Of course, everything that was slightly wet immediately froze — including leaves on the woods floor. The next two days were futile. My partners and I would walk into one end of a woods, and deer would immediately hear us and run out the other side. We were almost at our wit's end.

But then, during midmorning the fifth day, something miraculous happened. It started to snow — hard. The snow continued throughout the day and most of the night. When we awoke early Thanksgiving morning, more than 14 inches of white stuff blanketed the ground. Our group had wished for snow, but that was ridiculous. It seemed conditions had gone from one terrible extreme to something worse.

Five of us were in camp that day, and I think we deserve credit. We never considered spending the day in camp, and we began planning our strategy soon after daylight. We decided to make a series of leap-frog pushes through an expanse of 5-year-old regrowth. We knew the deep snow would make for tough going, so we decided to alternate pushers during each drive.

Typically, the drive to our hunting spot would have taken five minutes. Because of the deep snow, however, it took almost a half-hour. Many drifts were so deep that we had to take several runs at them before breaking through. Then, the vehicle would threaten to overheat, so we'd have to use another four-wheel drive vehicle to break the trail.

Success Right Away

My good friend Dan Dyson and I volunteered to push during the first drive. The standers, Paul and Dale Gumness and their dad, Emil, would take positions at strategic points about one-quarter mile ahead. When we reached them, Paul and Dale would stay to push the next chunk of regrowth. Meanwhile, Dan, Emil and I would circle around and stand another quarter-mile ahead. It was a simple plan, but it had worked well in the past.

Dan and I gave the standers plenty of time to get into position before beginning the push. I hadn't gone 20 yards before I cut a fresh set of huge deer tracks. Several yards farther, I found tracks from more deer. Soon, I stood amid a maze of tracks.

"This should be good," I whispered. "We're definitely going to run some deer out of this chunk of cover."

I'd walked about 100 yards farther when I heard a rifle shot ahead. Two more shots rang out seconds later, and then all was silent. Dan and I stayed put for two minutes before continuing. Fifteen minutes later, I saw a blaze orange-clad figure standing atop a tall ridge. It was Paul, and he was pointing urgently into the brush ahead of me. He had a deer down.

I learned later that Paul and Dale had filled their antlerless permits during the push. Thirty minutes later, we had field-dressed the deer and loaded them into Paul's truck. Then, it was time to implement Phase 2 of our plan. Emil and Dan jumped in my truck, and we took off for our stands.

Because of the deep snow and tough going, we left Emil to watch a good deer trail that crossed the logging road we were driving on. Dan and I then took a hard left on another logging trail and drove about 75 yards before stopping. We slogged another 75 yards through deep snow

I heard a driver shoot several times. We had no antlerless permits left, so I knew the shots were fired at a buck.

into the clear-cut and headed for a small rise. With the snowy background, Dan could cover lots of ground from the rise.

I pushed until the logging trail made a sharp right turn. I left the trail and walked into the clear-cut. My plan was to stand on a ridgetop overlooking the far southeastern corner of the clear-cut. A creek flowed through the area about 100 yards east, and many of the deer we'd pushed from the cover in the past — including most of the bucks — had traveled through the clear-cut valley before cutting east and crossing the creek. I would do my best to prevent that from happening.

I'd been at my stand less than a minute when I heard Paul indicate the push had begun. I hunkered deeper into my wool jacket and focused on a slight saddle to my right where deer often crossed as they headed for the creek bottom. I was so focused on watching the spot that I was somewhat startled by a volley of shots that suddenly echoed through the winter woods. Paul or Dale had fired the shots — or both! And because we had no antlerless permits left, I knew they were shooting at a buck.

Of course, I didn't know whether they had killed a buck. I'm convinced that made me more nervous. Instead of continuing to concentrate on the saddle crossing, I tried to watch 10 spots. Thankfully, I regained my senses and again focused on the saddle.

Minutes later, I detected a flash of movement in thick brush near the saddle. Seconds later, a big buck sauntered into view.

I slowly shouldered my .270 and found the whitetail in the scope. Just then, he made a sharp right turn and started easing toward me in thick brush below. The deer was coming closer, so I held off. However, when he was about 80 yards out, the buck suddenly turned left. He was headed for the creek crossing!

I locked the cross-hairs on the buck's vitals and let out a sharp, loud whistle. The deer instantly locked up. A split-second later, I launched a 130-grain missile. The recoil briefly rocked my vision, but I saw the buck do the double hind-leg kick characteristic of a fatally hit animal. He ran less than 50 yards before piling up in a shower of snow.

My partners and I knew we couldn't beat or match the results from the first two pushes, so we called it a day. We returned to the cabin — exhausted — by 2 p.m, and we had a large dinner cooking by 3 p.m.

Costly mistakes blew my chance at this buck during the early-archery season. Luckily, I had another chance during gun season.

That 1983 Thanksgiving meal was one of the most delicious and memorable I've eaten.

And what about the buck I'd killed? Well, I'm certain it was the alfalfa-field deer I'd hunted earlier that fall. His rack featured good tine length and an inside spread of slightly less than 19 inches. Further, he had that characteristic high rack.

However, one factor left no doubt. When I'd seen the buck opening weekend of archery season, he already sported his winter coat. Also, I'd noticed that his coat was unusually light. Instead of the slate-gray color common for whitetails in that part of Wisconsin, the buck's hide was light brown. The buck I shot Thanksgiving was also light brown.

What I Learned

The most obvious lesson from the hunt occurred the day I prepared my archery stand. It's easy to look back and recognize several blatant, costly mistakes I made that mid-September day. However, they weren't as obvious then. Remember, I only had a couple of years of somewhat serious trophy whitetail hunting experience.

I learned another valuable lesson from that 1983 Thanksgiving hunt: Never give up. The deep snow had prompted folks in most other deer camps to quit for the season. Our group was one of the few that stuck it out.

The final lesson, which I believe was the most important, involved deer movement. I knew whitetails — especially big bucks — occasionally wander from their home ranges, but I didn't know they'd travel so far. I killed the big 8-pointer more than two miles from the alfalfa field where I'd seen him in August and September.

Nowadays, of course, hunters know that a two-mile relocation isn't a big deal for a mature whitetail. However, that wasn't common knowledge in 1983. I filed away that tidbit along with other things I'd discovered the previous few seasons.

Slowly but surely, I was learning what made those wonderful creatures tick.

Rattling Works in the North, Too!

I continued to hone my hunting skills during archery and gun seasons in the mid-1980s. During that time, I had many memorable experiences, including a season-long bow-hunt for a big buck in 1985. That pursuit confirmed several aspects of rub-line behavior I hadn't substantiated previously, and those discoveries helped me pattern and kill a mature buck during the 1986 archery season.

Along the way, however, I overcame tremendous adversity.

Spring Scouting Proves its Worth

Think back several years. Did you scout during spring and the post-season in the mid-1980s, and did you spend several weeks each spring seeking shed antlers? I probably already know the answer: You weren't involved much — if at all — in either.

How do I know? Simple. My hunting partners and I spent loads of time hunting sheds and scouting during spring and the post-season during the mid-1980s. We never saw anyone else in the woods.

Interestingly, our scouting and shed-hunting occurred on public land. You'd think we would have encountered at least one other person, but we didn't. Why? Few hunters even knew about post-season or spring scouting. Fewer knew about hunting sheds.

That doesn't mean other folks weren't doing those things in the mid-1980s. They were just few and far between.

The up side, of course, was that my partners and I had the woods to ourselves during the off season. Better, we had no competition for sheds. That's a far cry from the situation today.

At first, Jeff and I couldn't figure out why the big bucks were rubbing and scraping so close to the road. However, we figured it out after a little more investigating.

One sunny, cool day in late March 1985, my brother Jeff and I were scouting a section of big woods in northwestern Wisconsin. We had learned about the spot while studying a topographical map. The chunk of timber featured a deep, slow-flowing creek and, based on what we'd seen, had the earmarks of a whitetail hotspot.

Jeff and I were in the woods less than five minutes when we started finding rubs on small, medium and large trees, including 10- to 12-inch-diameter spruces. We also found at least a dozen scrapes.

"There must have been two or three big bucks traveling through here regularly," I said. "I sure wish we'd have known about this last fall."

One thing puzzled us, however. Almost all the sign was near the town road where we'd parked our vehicle. At first, we couldn't determine why the big bucks had concentrated their rubbing and scraping near the road. However, the story became clear as we investigated further.

We had followed a wide expanse of high ground after leaving the road. However, as we walked deeper into the woods, the high ground became increasingly narrow. Two factors were responsible. First, the creek to our left, to which we had walked parallel, made a sudden, sharp bend to the east. Second, a large swamp to our right angled northwest. The result was a natural funnel.

Jeff and I continued to follow the ever-narrowing high ground until it was just 10 yards wide. The high ground then dropped off and disappeared where thick cover along the creek bottom met thick swamp cover. Jeff and I mulled the situation for seconds before plunging in. When we emerged from the swamp an hour later, we had found two buck bedding areas.

Like other serious trophy hunters, Jeff and I had high hopes for scouting missions. However, we never expected to discover such a gold mine. That day, we pinpointed the two hottest rub lines and found stand sites that would let us hunt the area during different wind conditions.

I didn't know it then, but that was our most important move.

Keeping Tabs on 'My Deer'

In a move that attests to his unselfish nature, Jeff said I should hunt our newly found hotspot. I didn't argue much. We knew that if we hunted the area properly, we'd have a chance at a big buck.

Although I'm extolling the virtues of off-season scouting, I've also learned that it has a drawback: It can be difficult to wait till the next season. That wait seems longer when you know you're sitting on a trophy whitetail hotspot. Summer, which passes slowly enough, crawls even more.

I developed a plan to help me deal somewhat with the slow summer of 1986. My family and I would spend almost every weekend at our northwestern Wisconsin cabin. My wife, Geralyn, enjoyed spending time up North, so my decision didn't cause friction. Also, my son, Jake, who was 2 at the time, loved the cabin. Looking back, I realize how precious and special those times were.

My plan was simple and easy to execute. While at the cabin, I'd get up before daylight and head to my new hunting area. Then, I'd slowly cruise the gravel town road that bordered the southern edge of the area. My main objective was to see a big buck — or bucks — crossing the road at first light. My second objective was to check the shoulder for fresh tracks. It was the best way to monitor deer activity in the area without disturbing bucks.

You might find this difficult to believe, but my simple summer scouting proved helpful — and not because of deer sightings, either. Though I often cruised through the area at prime time, I saw just two bucks all summer. However, they were legitimate shooters.

Actually, the many fresh deer tracks I found along the road edge stoked my fire and revealed valuable information. Unlike the does, fawns and small bucks that routinely crossed the road, the bigger bucks almost always crossed at a specific spot. Jeff and I hadn't paid much attention to that runway when we'd scouted the previous spring.

One Early Hunt, Then Out

I waited until the weekend before archery season opened before scouting the potential hotspot. Man, was I disappointed.

Besides looking for deer, I continually checked the road for fresh tracks. It was the best way to keep track of deer activity.

My short stint in the woods revealed little deer sign and no big buck sign. I decided to wait until midmorning opening day to place my stand in a tall, thick spruce Jeff and I had selected earlier that year. The tree was within easy range of two rub lines that had seen considerable buck traffic the previous year.

Because of something I call opening-day insanity, I returned to the stand three hours before dark. The first 2½ hours were uneventful. However, as the sun was about to set, I heard something in the thick brush to my right. I turned my head and saw a doe walking toward me. A fawn joined her seconds later.

I watched the deer as they moved slowly toward my stand. It soon became apparent they were feeding on something on the forest floor. At first, I thought they were eating acorns, but then I remembered there were no oaks in the area. My curiosity piqued, so I grabbed my binoculars and focused on the doe. The deer were eating mushrooms!

That wasn't the first time I'd seen whitetails eat mushrooms during the early archery season. Those experiences had taught me how difficult it was to pattern deer in mushroom-gobbling mode. Typically, mushrooms are scattered, and it's almost impossible to pattern deer that constantly feed at different locations.

Still, I learned something: It would probably be wise to avoid the area for a while. I had no doubts that at least one big buck was traveling through the area. However, I was sure most of that activity occurred after dark. Also, although my intrusions would be infrequent, there was a good chance the bucks would catch on to my plan. I wouldn't let that happen.

Fortunately, I had a ready excuse to avoid the area for at least a couple of weeks. For two years, I'd scrimped and saved for my first out-of-state whitetail bow-hunt with outfitter Russell Thornberry in southeastern Alberta.

The hunt was scheduled to run 10 days. However, after figuring in travel time, I'd be away from home for two weeks. I eagerly anticipated pointing my pickup northwest for Alberta.

But two days before I was scheduled to leave, disaster struck.

Almost Out of the Game

That morning began like any other during my construction career. I shut off the alarm at 5:30 a.m. and took a few minutes to stretch and wake up. I waited until my eyes really opened before swinging my legs out of bed. Everything seemed normal until I tried to stand. I never quite made it before collapsing on the floor. Judging from the agonizing pain shooting up the lower part of my left leg, something was terribly wrong.

Geralyn came to my side immediately. With her help, I got up and sat on the edge of the bed. The intense pain subsided in minutes.

"I don't know what the heck that was all about, but it was kind of scary," I said. "Let's go have a cup of coffee, and I'll see how I feel when it's time to go to work."

I went to work, but had only been on the job two hours when the intense pain in my left leg returned. It was even scarier, because it

I hunted the area once in the early season, and then stayed away until the late pre-rut in hopes that resident bucks wouldn't figure out my game plan.

Many mule deer occupied the ranch, which was a welcome diversion. I killed a decent 5-by-4 toward the end of my hunt.

didn't go away. However, I had a good idea what was happening.

More than two years before, I'd undergone surgery to replace a worn joint in my left foot with an artificial joint. I had no doubt the pain in my leg stemmed from the artificial joint in my foot.

I ended up in the emergency room. The doctor who had performed the surgery arrived minutes later. He listened as I described my problem, and then immediately ordered X-rays of my left foot. When he returned, I could tell he didn't have good news.

"Your body is rejecting the artificial joint we put in your foot a couple of years ago," he said. "The intense pain you're feeling is caused by a serious infection that's actually eating away the bone on either side of the joint."

As if that wasn't bad enough, he continued.

"This is a fairly serious situation," he said. "I want you back at this hospital at 7 a.m. tomorrow to be prepped for surgery. I'm going to have to go in and take out that artificial joint. You might want to let your employer know that you're going to be laid up for a while. At this point, I can't really say for sure how long it will be before you're fully recovered."

I can be a bit bullheaded sometimes, and that was one of those times.

"For two years, I've been planning my first out-of-state bow-hunt," I said, looking the doctor in the eye. "I'm scheduled to leave for that hunt the day after tomorrow. Doc, I will be going on that hunt! But I give you my word that I'll be here at the hospital at 7:30 a.m. the day after I get back. You can do the surgery then."

Amazingly, he only argued mildly. However, he made me promise I'd take massive doses of antibiotics during my two-week trip. He also prescribed strong pain medication. Then, we shook hands.

"I'll see you back here exactly two weeks from today," he said. "Good luck."

The next two weeks passed incredibly fast. Although the whitetails refused to play, my bow-hunt with Thornberry was unforgettable. The ranch we hunted also held lots of mule deer, which proved a welcome diversion (Thornberry had insisted that I also purchase a mule deer tag). Late one afternoon, a bachelor group of five muley bucks wandered within range, and I arrowed a decent 5-by-4.

Then, I returned home for my date with the surgeon. My foot hadn't caused much trouble while I was in Alberta. I'd gotten around well and even slept through most nights. But things changed dramatically during the drive home. The intense pain I'd experienced before the hunt surfaced again. I never thought I'd look forward to going to a hospital — until Oct. 13, 1986.

A Disturbing Prognosis

What was supposed to be a 90-minute surgery lasted more than three hours. The bone-eating infection around the artificial joint was considerably worse than the X-rays had indicated. As a precautionary measure, the surgeon left the incision in my foot open until he received conclusive findings about the infection, samples of which he had sent to a lab at another hospital. The findings arrived two days later, and I was soon back in the operating room. The surgeon had to fuse the bone from my big toe with the bone in the top of my foot. Because the joint between the bones had been removed, the big toe on my left foot ended up more than an inch shorter than normal.

After the second surgery, I had to spend at least two more days in the hospital. Also, I had to be on crutches for at least two weeks.

Of course, I made some quick calculations. If everything went well, I might get in some bow-hunts before the season closed.

Goodbye to Crutches

I used the crutches religiously the first several days after being released. The next few days, I walked with them more often than not. Finally, a week after leaving the hospital, I got rid of them. I was in the woods the next day.

Sure, my foot still hurt a bit. In fact, the usually routine task of pulling my rubber boot onto my left foot brought tears to my eyes. Also, I had to deal with the side effects of being anesthetized twice in three days. I was weak and also experienced occasional bouts of light-headedness. I quickly learned that too much exertion pushed me to the brink of blacking out.

However, adversity wouldn't prevent me from hunting. It was that magical time of the year when bucks were madly scraping and rubbing. I knew the hotspot Jeff and I had found the previous spring would be rocking and rolling. It was.

During midmorning Oct. 26, I quickly walked through the funnel. As I suspected, there was buck sign everywhere. I placed a portable tree stand near a hot rub line and headed out. I almost passed out twice during the short walk to my truck. Putting up the stand had been more taxing than I'd realized.

But the tough part was finished — so I thought.

Rattling Works

More than two hours of daylight remained when I climbed into my stand. I couldn't help but be excited. The weather was overcast and cool, with a slight northeast breeze. I planned to wait 30 minutes and try a strategy that was relatively new to that area: Using rattling antlers to entice a big buck from one of the bedding areas in the swamp. I figured I had nothing to lose.

I was optimistic my strategy would work. However, I never dreamed I'd receive such an immediate, positive response. I was just halfway through my first rattling sequence when I heard a loud, aggressive grunt somewhere in the swamp. Seconds later, I heard a buck battling a clump of brush. Then, another loud grunt emanated from the swamp. That let me zero in on the buck.

Soon, I heard a deer walking, and I could tell it was heading toward me. I grabbed my bow, quickly nocked an arrow and clipped the release to the string. The buck only had to walk out of the thick tamarack swamp to provide a decent shot. However, that part of the plan wouldn't come together just yet.

Twenty-five minutes later, I was still ready, but the buck hadn't appeared. I knew he was still heading toward me, though. Every few minutes, the buck would utter a loud, challenging grunt. He had also thrashed the daylights out of several trees along the way. Obviously, the deer was still mighty interested in the buck fight he'd heard ear-

My hunting partners and I were actively involved in scouting in the mid-1980s, including scouring the woods for shed antlers.

lier. However, he wouldn't rush in to investigate.

A half-hour elapsed before I finally saw movement near the edge of the swamp 30 yards away. I saw the legs of a deer and then a body. Suddenly, a dandy 10-point buck strode out of the swamp. What a sight! His ears were back, and the hair atop his neck and back stood on end like that of a mad dog. That buck was ready to battle.

He walked to a clump of tag alders, dropped his head and provided a classic display of aggressive rubbing. Then, he abruptly stopped and jerked his head erect. Stems of long yellow grass and several small branches adorned the buck's antlers — but only briefly. With a quick shake of his head, the buck rid his antlers of adornment. Then, he issued another loud grunt and again started walking toward me.

The 10-pointer closed within 10 yards before stopping to study his surroundings. However, he was facing me, so I couldn't shoot.

Things got worse. The buck figured out that something wasn't right. Rather than turning right or left, though, he did a quick about-face and began walking toward the swamp. He was facing away from me, so again I couldn't shoot.

The buck continued to slowly walk away. I thought the game was finished and that I'd lost — but that's when I received a pleasant surprise. The buck eventually reached the hot rub line that coursed along the swamp edge, and instead of continuing into the swamp, he suddenly turned right and began easing along the rub line. He was broadside.

The shot was relatively easy. The big-bodied whitetail was only 25 yards away when the arrow zipped through his vitals. He took three dainty bounds into the swamp before stopping to look back. He tipped over dead seconds later.

What I Learned

I learned one of my most unforgettable — and unpleasant — lessons when I tried to drag the 10-pointer out of the swamp. I got the deer to high ground, but that's as far as I made it before passing out. I don't know how long I was out. It might have only been a minute. Regardless, it convinced me I'd need help dragging the deer from the woods. Also, I knew I was far from healed.

Of course, the hunt also provided a couple of other lessons. The most significant was that you can rattle in big bucks in the North Woods. Since then, I've also rattled in mature bucks in many other states. Nowadays, most serious whitetail hunters know that rattling antlers and grunt calls are important items.

The other lesson concerned off-season scouting. My success was attributable to a day of intense scouting — even though it occurred almost seven months before the hunt.

That only reinforced the importance of hitting the woods during spring and after the season.

Hunting With
a Special Friend

It had been a long, tough hunt. Guide Shane Hansen and I had spent the week seeking a big Alberta whitetail. We had fought through endless tangles of thick brush, trudged over countless hills and walked dozens of miles. Those tasks were more difficult because of 10 inches of fresh snow.

Except for the first couple of days, we had been afield before daylight till after dusk — more than 10 hours — each day, trying to kill a big buck.

Although we had seen some big deer, I hadn't fired a shot.

A Gracious Invitation

That Alberta trip was my second to the province during Fall 1986. The first trip, a bow-hunt for whitetails and mule deer in southeastern Alberta, had occurred six weeks earlier. Outfitter Russell Thornberry had worked hard to get my partner and me within range of trophy whitetails, but it never happened. Had it not been for the many mule deer on the ranch, the trip would have been uneventful.

No one was more disappointed than Thornberry. In fact, he was so disturbed that he extended a gracious invitation after our bow-hunt.

"You know, I have a couple of openings at my gun-hunting operation the first week of November," he said. "If you guys can make it work, I'd like to have you come back and hunt with me then. All it will cost you is your air fare."

We were speechless, because Thornberry operated one of the best whitetail operations in Alberta. Getting the chance to chase big bucks with someone like him for almost 10 days was like winning the lottery. We immediately said we'd find a way to return in November.

Then, however, I remembered something. As detailed in Chapter 8, I had to undergo surgery immediately after I returned to Wisconsin.

"Don't worry, Greg," Thornberry said. "We'll find a way to get you out in the woods. Just keep in touch and let me know how you're doing, and we'll go from there. If you can get around at all after the surgery, we should be able to put you in position to get a crack at a good buck."

I came through the surgery fairly well. In fact, less than two weeks later, I was hunting. Other than being somewhat weak and occasionally light-headed, I was recovering well.

I just couldn't push myself too hard in Canada.

I Meet Hansen

On Oct. 31, my partner and I returned to Alberta. We flew to Edmonton and met a friend of Thornberry's at the airport. After a three-hour drive, we reached Thornberry's camp near the Battle River in western Alberta. He was standing in the yard when we pulled up. We shook hands, and then Thornberry introduced me to Hansen, my guide for the hunt.

Hansen helped me carry my gear inside, and then told me to put on warmer clothes.

"I want you to shoot your rifle a couple of times to make sure it's still zeroed in," he said. "After we're done, we'll drive around, and I'll show you some of the country we'll be hunting the next few days."

Before our arrival, the weather had been warmer and drier than normal, creating poor hunting conditions. However, things were about to change for the better.

While sighting in our guns, we noticed the air was getting colder. When we returned to the lodge, a light snow was falling. That night

The first trip would have been uneventful if not for the many mule deer at the Alberta ranch.

I saw and passed up several fairly large bucks the next few days, and I almost shot a long-tined 10-pointer.

and through the next day, a snowstorm raged.

And just before dark the first day, I had my first encounter with a mature Alberta whitetail.

To Shoot or Not to Shoot?

The heavy snowfall made conditions tough. Hansen and I spent several hours watching a buck crossing that morning. During midday, Hansen made several pushes through some small patches of cover. The only deer we saw was a 2½-year-old 8-pointer, which got our hearts racing — but for the wrong reasons. The buck suddenly burst from some timber and almost struck Hansen's truck.

A half-hour of daylight remained when we found fresh tracks from a big buck in a wheat field. Hansen quickly sized up the situation and pointed to some timber.

"I'll bet he went into that patch of bush," he said. "Let's drive over there and see if he came out the other side."

We drove around the woods, but found no tracks coming out of the woodlot. Minutes later, Hansen stopped where the buck had entered the woods.

"Grab your gun and sneak back around to the wheat field on the other side of this woods," he said. "I'll give you a few minutes, and then I'm going to come through on the buck's trail. With any luck, he'll bust out somewhere in front of you."

It seemed like a good plan, and it would have worked. However, the buck threw a wrench in the works: He had already walked through the timber. I was easing around a corner when I saw him, standing alone at the edge of the wheat field about 100 yards away.

I shouldered my rifle and found the buck in the scope. His body was huge, but I couldn't determine the size of his antlers. The raging snowfall and rapidly fading daylight didn't help. Also, the buck's head was obscured by thick brush in the background. I just couldn't determine how much of what I saw was antlers and how much was brush.

I didn't get more time, either. The buck saw me when he heard Hansen walking along his trail. He spooked and ran hard across the wheat field. I watched the buck through the scope, which had become peppered with snowflakes. It was impossible to analyze his antlers, so I had to let the deer go.

I thought Hansen would be disappointed, but he was relieved that I hadn't killed the deer.

"I don't want you to shoot unless you're absolutely sure," he said. "Besides, it's only the first day of the hunt. We've got lots of time to find you a good buck. And this snow is going to help, too."

Lots of Hours, Miles

To increase our time afield, Hansen and I quit returning to the lodge for lunch after the second day.

"As far as I'm concerned, we're just wasting valuable hunting time," he said.

I agreed. Afterward, we left the lodge before daylight and didn't return till after dark. The routine proved physically and mentally exhausting.

I saw and passed up several big bucks the next few days. In fact, I almost shot a wide-racked, long-tined 10-pointer. I'd already pushed off the safety and was starting to squeeze the trigger when Hansen whispered that I shouldn't shoot.

"That's a pretty good buck," I replied.

"Yeah, he is pretty good," Hansen said. "But we can do better. We've still got some time left."

I was extremely upset that Hansen had called me off. I became quiet and disinterested, tipping him off that I was boiling inside.

"I know you wanted to shoot that buck, Greg," he said. "But I really don't think you would have been happy with him. I promise you, I will get you a chance at a bigger buck."

The next three days were almost a replay of the first three. I saw and passed up several more bucks. However, those decisions were much easier because the deer were obvious 2½-year-olds, featuring stout bodies but just average racks.

A New Game Plan

During the seventh day, Hansen decided to try something new.

Twenty-five yards from the hot scrape, we saw a fresh rub on a 4-inch-diameter tree. We knew where we'd hunt for the rest of my trip.

"The Battle River should be frozen hard enough to support our weight," he said. "We're going to wait until about noon, and then we're going to cross the river and do some poking around in the breaks on the other side. Nobody has touched any of that country yet, and I'd be surprised if there aren't a bunch of big bucks hanging out over there."

His assessment proved correct. In little more than an hour, we found so much buck sign it was absurd. After walking more, we realized we'd found a rare situation: There was actually too much sign. Unless we found something incredible, it would be difficult to decide where to set up.

We checked a final spot and hit pay dirt: a steaming-hot scrape under a low-hanging branch of a stunted, gnarly poplar in a small meadow. Obviously, several big bucks were using the scrape as a primary scent station. Numerous fresh tracks led to the scrape from every direction. Twenty-five yards from the scrape, we saw a fresh rub on a 4-inch-diameter tree. Hansen and I knew immediately where we'd hunt the rest of my trip.

We soon found a spot that provided a good view of the scrape and kept the wind in our favor. Then, we set up and began our vigil. However, as promising as the area appeared, we knew it would take luck for a buck to visit the scrape that evening. We had stomped around too much the previous two hours.

The second time we walked the mile-long walk to the scrape, the wind suddenly switched, blowing from our ambush site to the scrape.

"No sense setting up here," Hansen said disgustedly. "If a buck comes in, he'll smell us and be gone before you can get a shot."

A Shooter Shows Up

We quickly formed an alternate plan. Basically, we would walk slowly, peering into fields and power-line cuts in hopes of catching a big buck moving.

"We've got a couple of hours until dark," Hansen said. "Let's make a circle around this woodlot behind us and then slowly start making our way back to the truck."

After 90 minutes and a 1-mile walk, we sneaked down a power-line cut bordered by timber on one side and open pasture on the other. We were about to descend a steep hill when a doe bolted from the timber and ran across the power-line cut. She jumped a four-strand barbwire fence, trotted into the pasture and then stopped to stare into the woods.

"Sneak over to that fence post and get ready to shoot, Greg!" Hansen said. "She's acting like there might be a buck behind her."

Just as I reached the post and settled my Ruger .270, I saw a buck coming. The deer was heading toward the power-line cut with his head down. Almost as quickly, he crossed the opening, jumped the fence and slowed to a trot about 225 yards away.

"He's a good buck, Greg! Go ahead and take him!" Hansen said excitedly.

I centered the deer in the scope, followed him for several steps and squeezed the trigger. The first shot kicked up snow inches over his back. I had swung level on a deer moving slightly downhill. Duh! As the shot echoed through the Battle River breaks, the buck stopped to see what was happening. The second bullet killed him. We watched the deer pile up after a ground-hugging 100-yard dash. Hansen turned to me and smiled.

"Nice shot," he said triumphantly. "Let's walk over and take a closer look at your buck."

The setting couldn't have been more perfect or picturesque. The buck died atop a hill that overlooked much of the beautiful Battle River breaks. Hansen and I knelt in the snow next to the big white-tail, not speaking for several seconds. However, seconds later, we couldn't shut up, and babbled nonstop about how quickly events had transpired. Less than 30 seconds had passed from when we'd seen the doe till the fatal shot. However, my memories of the hunt would last forever.

The buck sported six typical tines on one side of his rack and five on the other. The rack's inside spread was just wider than 18 inches, and the main beams were almost 25 inches. Except for stubby brow

Killing a 150-class whitetail is reason enough to be happy. However, the outcome was sweeter because of the effort it took to get within range of a shooter buck.

tines, the rack had good tine length throughout. It gross-scored in the low 150s.

One of my favorite memories occurred a couple of hours later, when Thornberry clasped my hand in congratulations. Killing a fine Alberta buck was reason enough to be happy, but that only partly explained my exuberance. The outcome was sweeter because of the energy Hansen and I had expended just to find a shooter buck.

Some Lessons

As I'd done during Wisconsin's bow season two weeks earlier, I learned I still hadn't recovered from my surgery. The day after shooting the 11-pointer, I contracted what I thought was a bad cold. When I arrived home days later, however, I realized it was more. The doctor later told me I had a severe case of pneumonia. The surgery and the exhausting eight days I spent with Hansen had finally caught up to me.

It's amazing what hunters will do sometimes to get a big buck. I'm sure you can relate.

Still, my success in Alberta was the direct result of the hard work Hansen and I put in. The results convinced me that I couldn't accelerate my success with big bucks.

Time and sweat meant more than any other factor.

Until Next Year

I've hunted many bucks through the years, and each has provided cherished memories.

You might think my largest bucks have provided my fondest memories, but that's not true. My deer hunting memories have never — and will never — be ranked according to antler size.

In the next two chapters, I'll detail one of my most memorable hunts. It requires two chapters because the hunt spanned almost two years. I first hunted the mature North Woods buck in Fall 1988 and didn't close the deal till November 1989.

That buck, although respectable, didn't sport monstrous antlers. However, he had intelligence, cunning and a sixth sense that still impresses me. No matter what I did, the deer was always one step ahead.

The Hunt Begins

Except for hissing logs in the fireplace, my cabin was silent. I stood and stared at the burning embers for several seconds. It had been a long season. Three months earlier, I began pursuing the monster buck I planned to hunt that evening.

We knew each other well. His ability to stay a step ahead had kept him alive. However, the game would quickly end, because it was the final day of archery season.

The warm, pleasant days of September and October were forgotten, replaced by the harsh early-winter cold of December. It had been minus 15 the previous evening and minus 10 the evening before that.

I had no desire to shoot the small deer, so I watched as it fed within range for 30 minutes.

I checked the thermometer outside the cabin: minus 12.

That was OK. I was becoming accustomed to the cold — or maybe just learning to deal with it.

A Frigid Ritual

Slowly, I began the ritual of layering my clothing. I knew I'd have at least a two-hour wait before — if — the buck appeared. My apparel had to be warm but not restrictive. Experience from many seasons in frigid conditions served me well. I began with long underwear, added a layer of thermals and donned wool atop that. I put light socks on my feet and topped them with two pairs of wool socks. Heavy Canadian pac-type boots, designed for extreme cold, engulfed my sock-encased feet. Then, I pulled on down-filled mittens, which I could remove quickly and quietly at crucial moments. I placed insulated coveralls in my backpack, which I'd don just before climbing into my stand.

After finishing, I hesitated. My mind drifted back to a cool, frosty October morning. I had been on stand near where I planned to hunt that evening. The buck had walked through out of range, reducing me to a spectator in nature's game. Still, I wondered, is there a sight as grand as a huge whitetail buck, unaware of your presence, being himself?

His body was massive, and he hadn't yet lost weight from chasing does. And what antlers! He sported 10 long, evenly matched points and main beams as fat as my wrist. That buck was a grand specimen.

As quickly as the deer had appeared, though, he vanished, swallowed by brush. It made no difference. I had seen enough to be hooked. I frequented that area the next few weeks and, after the big boy began rubbing and scraping, got a better idea about his movements.

Back to the Present

I was jolted back to reality by the pop of dry oak in the fireplace. It was time to head out.

My nostrils almost froze as I stepped into the cold. I wondered how much someone would have to pay me to hunt if a big whitetail wasn't involved.

The drive to my hunting area was less than a mile. I parked my truck, grabbed my gear and started the quarter-mile walk to my stand. Plodding along, I noticed the cold snow squeaking underfoot.

I reached my tree and saw several fresh deer tracks nearby. There was no mistaking one set: the wide, splayed print of the buck. So, he had passed through here after I left the previous night. I was optimistic he'd appear earlier that night. My stand was near a prime feeding area, and the cold would surely prompt him to restore his depleted fat reserves.

I pulled the insulated coveralls from my backpack and put them on. My gloveless hands tingled from the cold during the brief climb into my stand. After pulling up my bow, I nocked an arrow and practiced drawing twice to ensure my bulky clothing didn't interfere with shooting. I checked to ensure everything was OK with my bow, and then hung it on a dead limb.

Settling in, I prepared for a motionless vigil. The day before, I had found the shed antler of a small buck on a nearby runway. Then, the little deer, with frozen blood hanging from his right pedicel, walked under me. With no desire to shoot him, I had watched as he browsed within range for almost 30 minutes. That helped the time pass. Would he return to entertain me?

Recalling November

A half-hour after settling in, my thoughts returned to the big buck. I remembered an early-November morning when he almost made a fatal mistake.

A doe had appeared, and I knew a buck would follow. With her mouth hanging open and tail tucked tightly, the doe had left no doubt she was in estrus. I had soon heard the buck coming, busting brush and emitting deep-pitched grunts.

The doe had looked back toward the buck and trotted toward me, passing within 10 yards.

"This is it," I had thought. "He's going to follow right in her tracks and give me a shot."

It had seemed too easy.

Everything had been fine. My dream buck had been walking along, head down, following the doe's trail. If he had taken a few more steps, I would have had a perfect shot. But suddenly, he had stopped, snapped his head up and looked toward me. I dared not breath. I soon realized he wasn't looking at me but knew something was amiss.

Instead of continuing, the buck had turned and taken five quick steps to his right. He got behind a blowdown and stopped 25 yards away, but I could only see his huge rack and one eye peering through dead branches. Shooting had been out of the question.

Five minutes had passed, and then 10. The buck had moved nothing but his head, trying to pinpoint the danger. I had waited for him to emerge from the blowdown, giving me a clear shot. If he turned and walked away, keeping the blowdown between us, he would be safe.

The big monarch hadn't panicked or acted nervous. He just turned and walked away. When he had walked about 30 yards, he stopped and looked back. What a sight! His neck was swollen to absurd size, and his antlers had been polished to mahogany brown: the epitome of a rutting buck.

After 15 seconds, the deer had trotted off, tail held high. He had won that round.

I had collapsed on my stand seat, exhausted. Although I had been there only an hour, I left. It would have been impossible to hunt longer.

Time Flies

My mind returned to the present. Glancing at my watch, I was surprised that more than an hour had passed. So far, the cold hadn't bothered me, other than causing a perpetually runny nose.

The little buck had appeared at about the same time the previous day. Not that day, though. I wondered whether I'd spooked him by climbing down from my stand when he was nearby. If so, had I

The big buck stepped behind a blowdown and stopped 25 yards away. I could only see his rack and one eye, but a shot was out of the question.

tipped off the big buck?

After all, the big buck had also disappeared during the nine-day gun-hunt. Fearing that he had been shot, I had spent days searching for sign. Finally, a week before, during Christmas Eve, I found something better: I saw him at the food source near my stand.

The wind had been blowing hard from the buck toward me, and he was browsing with his head in the brush. I had never been so close to a mature buck that was so unaware of me. Later, I had paced off the distance at 35 yards. Of course, my bow was in the truck, because I was just checking for sign. I hadn't expected to see him, because it was midday.

He was alive. My fears were erased.

The buck had looked at me once, but I stayed motionless. Convinced he had nothing to fear, the deer had resumed feeding, and I slowly walked away. When I was out of sight, I had quickly walked to the truck, grabbed my bow and returned to the woods.

He was gone.

The buck's winter turf was a small corner of a huge chunk of land. Undoubtedly, gun-hunters had poked and prodded every inch of his stomping grounds except that 40-acre parcel. I was sure he'd spent the entire gun season there. But I'd found him.

However, finding and killing him were different. After seeing him Christmas Eve, I had hunted many hours without another sighting. Still, his huge, fresh tracks continued to appear near my stand. I figured it was just a matter of time before he appeared during shooting hours.

But was there enough left of the season?

Reappearing Act

So, there I was: The last day of the season. After almost two hours of waiting and watching, I hadn't seen the 10-pointer.

But suddenly, like magic, there he was.

Seconds earlier, there had been nothing. But mysteriously, he had appeared. He slowly turned his head, surveying his surroundings. It was him, no doubt. His tremendous body looked black against the snow. Even at 75 yards, I easily saw his heavy, long-tined rack. Shucking my heavy mittens, I grabbed my bow and got positioned for a shot. Just then, the buck began walking toward me.

It was going to happen — I just knew it!

At 40 yards, he stopped and looked around. He stuck his nose into the air and sucked in the wind currents. Satisfied the coast was clear, he dropped his head and continued toward me. My heart hammered like a bass drum inside my ears.

After coming within 20 yards, he stopped again and seemed to be staring at me. To avert his eyes and thwart his sixth sense, I shut my eyes. It worked. Again, he dropped his head and walked closer. A hundred thoughts rushed through my head.

"How big are his antlers? No doubt they'll easily make Pope and Young. Boy, his mounted head will look great on my wall! I wonder if someone is around to help track and drag him out. Should I draw now?"

Suddenly, the bucked stopped at 15 yards and snapped up his head, looking into my eyes. That wasn't in the plan. My gloveless hand began to go numb. I considered trying to draw while the buck stared at me, but I quickly dismissed that. It wouldn't have worked.

More time passed. My bow hand went from numb to nothing. Still, I persisted. If the buck turned his head to look away, I might be able to draw and shoot. It had been too long a season to give up.

Three or four minutes passed, and I knew I was in trouble. No longer worried about drawing my bow, my No. 1 concern was whether I could safely descend from my stand. My hands seemed detached from my arms — they were that cold. Still, I couldn't move or do anything to scare the deer. It went against everything I knew to intentionally spook a big buck away from my stand.

No Choices Remain

Finally, I had no choice.

"You win this time," I said, looking at the buck.

Instantly, the deer wheeled around and bounded away. Dejected, I sat and tried to warm my hands — a slow, painful process.

At 40 yards, the buck stopped and looked around. He stuck his nose into the air and sniffed the currents.

There he was, 60 yards away, watching. We had another brief staredown, and then he turned and walked away.

Eventually, enough feeling and mobility returned for me to climb down safely. I gathered my gear and began to walk out, but something compelled me to look back.

There he was, 60 yards away, watching. In the fading daylight, we had a brief staredown. Then, the buck turned and walked away. I watched till he disappeared, feeling the hollowness of being so close but coming up empty.

For some reason, I hollered at the buck.

"You're the winner," I shouted. "Until next year!"

What I Learned
First, I realized it doesn't take long for exposed flesh to freeze at minus 15. Also, I discovered that freezing your hands doesn't hurt as much as thawing them.

And as I mentioned previously, there's a huge difference between seeing a big buck and killing him. During all my seasons, I'd never seen a buck so often.

Of course, those sightings provided clues about how the buck moved through his home range. Unfortunately, it wasn't until that final encounter that I began piecing together the puzzle.

And I was eagerly anticipating the 1989 season.

Next Year

In the previous chapter, I detailed my season-long pursuit of a big North Woods buck. This chapter chronicles my hunts for that buck the next season.

Remarkably, time hasn't dulled my memories from the two-year pursuit, although it occurred almost 15 years ago. I still recall almost every detail of the hunt.

I've chased bigger deer, but this hunt remains one of my all-time favorites.

Another Encounter

I don't know what made me look over my left shoulder. Perhaps it was a sixth sense, honed by countless hours pursuing whitetails. Maybe it was because I know better than to concentrate too much in one direction. Too many lost chances have taught me that deer — especially mature bucks — seem to appear where they "ain't supposed to be."

The buck had already walked past and was quartering away when I saw him. Three inches of fresh snow let the big deer walk silently 20 yards behind my stand. I was lucky to have glanced that way. The buck was unlucky because if he'd moved faster, he would have reached thick cover before I turned.

Heavy clouds were rapidly dissipating, giving way to a clear sky. Soft midmorning sunlight filtered through the trees, illuminating small patches of the woodlot. As I shouldered my .270, the buck stepped into a patch of sunlight. His rack, which had first seemed dull and dark against the snow, seemed to glisten.

"I know this buck!" I thought.

The deer suddenly stopped, head erect, listening for any threat. Peering intently through the scope, I was ready. However, my eye wandered briefly from the kill zone to his antlers, confirming my suspicion.

It was him.

I couldn't mistake those antlers. I had seen them too often the past two years: long beams, a wide spread and at least 10 points. Plus, the deer had a huge body and was thick through the chest and neck. And rather than the slate-gray color of most North Woods bucks, he had a rusty hue.

I snapped back to reality. The buck resumed walking toward a small opening. I moved the rifle slightly, aligning the cross hairs in the opening. The buck's rack appeared, and his neck and chest followed. After one more step, I saw a shoulder. I centered the cross hairs and fired. The recoil obscured my vision momentarily, but when I recovered, the buck was down. As I chambered another round, however, the deer suddenly sprang up and was gone. I waited, rifle ready, hoping to see him moving through the underbrush.

Nothing. No sound, no movement — no buck.

After five minutes, I climbed down and slowly walked to where the buck had fallen. Blood and hair littered the snow. Staggering, running tracks led into thick cover. Even without snow, it would have been easy to see the deer was well hit. There was no need to push the issue, because the buck wouldn't go far.

Breathing a sigh of relief, I leaned against a giant poplar and recalled the events of the past two seasons.

The First Sighting

My mind returned to a cool October morning the previous year, when I first saw the buck. He had been out of range and wouldn't come closer. I had guessed him at 250 pounds, and his antlers matched his giant body: 10 even points adorned a dark, long-beamed rack. The deer had gazed at me for almost five minutes but

I felt no need to press the buck because it was hit hard. Breathing a sigh of relief, I relaxed.

After a long wait, the buck turned and walked away, with his huge, swollen neck accenting his majestic rack.

suddenly disappeared.

I had seen the deer again three weeks later, after he followed a hot doe — a move that almost killed him. As the doe approached, fleeing the buck's advances, I heard him coming, busting brush, breaking branches and grunting with every step, making no attempt to conceal his approach.

The doe had looked toward the buck once and trotted past me at 10 yards. I quickly got into shooting position and waited.

The buck had continued coming, but suddenly stopped. He raised his head and looked toward me. I didn't twitch, but he knew something was wrong and quickly moved behind a blowdown, where he stayed for 10 minutes, moving nothing but his head. If he had walked to either side, I would have had a shot.

After a while, the buck turned and slowly walked away, keeping the blowdown between us. At 30 yards, he had stopped and looked back, making me wish I had a camera instead of a bow. His huge, swollen neck accented his dark rack, providing a perfect example of a rutting buck.

He had posed for about 15 seconds, turned and trotted out of sight.

The Wait

Hearing someone walking through the brush, I snapped back to the present. It was longtime hunting companion Dan Dyson. Quietly, he asked what I had shot. Before I spoke, he seemed to know the answer. He knew about my pursuit of the buck.

"It was him, Dan," I said. "He almost got away again. I turned my head just in time to see him sneaking toward this thick brush behind me."

Dan glanced at the blood and hair.

"From the looks of this, I'd say the chase might finally be over," he said.

I nodded.

"I think we should wait a while before taking up the track, though," I said.

141

Dan agreed, and we stood silently. He knew what was going through my mind.

I thought about the late archery season the previous year, which I detailed in Chapter 10. The 10-pointer had remained hidden through the gun season but suddenly reappeared in December. I had walked up on the buck while scouting on Christmas Eve — without my bow. The next morning, I had sneaked back in and put up a stand.

Six afternoons of subzero temperatures passed before I saw him again, during the season's final minutes. He had approached within 20 yards but stopped. Soon, he dropped his head and walked closer.

Just as he had begun to turn broadside, he stopped again and looked at me. We exchanged stares. I was numb from cold, forcing me to move.

I told him he'd won, and he bolted. After I had climbed down, I saw him again at a distance. Before leaving, I told him I'd be back next year.

Next Year Arrives

Next year had arrived, and the red evidence in the snow indicated the buck might have made a fatal mistake. Dan saw me looking at the blood.

"Think we should go after him now?" he said.

"Let's give him a few more minutes," I said without raising my head.

A month earlier, I had been confident the buck was mine. The rut was just starting, so I brought rattling antlers to my bow stand one morning. About 30 minutes after getting settled, I had performed a 45-second rattling sequence, and before I hung up the antlers, I heard a deer approaching.

When the buck appeared, I had decided not to shoot. It was a little 8-pointer. The deer remained nearby for almost five minutes, looking for the fighting deer he had heard. Before leaving, he walked to the edge of a grassy swamp and looked toward a small spruce stand 50 yards away. I had followed his line of sight and almost lost

After approaching within 20 yards, the buck suddenly stopped. Soon, he dropped his head and walked closer.

I followed the little buck's line of sight and almost lost my breath. There was the big buck, standing knee deep in swamp grass.

my breath. There was the buck, standing knee deep in the frost-covered grass.

I thought he would come right to me. After all, he had obviously come to the rattling and seen a buck under my tree. Surely, I had thought, he would check whether the little buck had been fighting over a sweet-smelling doe.

I stared at the big buck as twin columns of steam billowed from his nostrils in the frosty morning air. He glared at the 8-pointer, and the small buck turned and skulked away, intimidated.

"This is great," I thought at the time. "That big guy is going to come over here and run off this small buck."

It didn't happen, though. The monster had watched just long enough to see the subordinate leave. Then, he turned and melted into the spruce. Light rattling and grunting couldn't coax him back.

I never saw him again during bow season. Still, huge rubs continued to appear almost daily, persuading me to hunt the area during gun season. I had discovered the buck's haunts, and his favorite pocket of cover attracted little hunting pressure.

I hunted him off and on during the gun season's first four days, but only when conditions were perfect. It was 9:30 a.m. the fifth day when he finally walked by.

If not for that casual glance over my shoulder, my hunt might have stretched to a third year.

Time to End It

Finally, I broke the silence.

"We've given him enough time, Dan," I said. "Why don't you circle around the patch of brush he ran into, just in case he isn't hit as hard as we think. I'll give you a few minutes to find a place to set up."

Dan nodded and walked off. The many hours we've shared in the woods have created an often-unspoken understanding. Sometimes, Dan can anticipate my moves, and vice versa. I waited 10 minutes for Dan to get into position, and then eased ahead on the buck's trail.

At first, the wounded deer made fairly large bounds. After 50 yards, however, he had slowed to a walk.

It's impossible to describe my feelings as I admired the buck. However, I realized that killing the deer didn't mean I had won the game.

About 25 yards farther, I saw him lying under a small white oak in a tiny clearing. His head was up, but he didn't look at me as I approached. Death was near.

Quickly, I shouldered my .270 and finished the deer with a neck shot.

Walking to the deer, I felt a great sense of accomplishment. I had waited two years for that moment. Kneeling, I grabbed an antler and slowly lifted his head from the snow. Apparently, age had made his rack somewhat stubby. Also, he had grown an extra tine on the right side, making him an 11-pointer.

I admired him for a few moments and set his head back on the snow.

After a while, I heard a soft, low whistle. Dan wanted to know what was going on. I didn't answer immediately, because I needed to be alone with the buck a few more minutes. Removing my gloves, I ran my hand over his beautiful rust-brown coat, smoothing the hair where it was ruffled by the brush.

The elation I initially felt was replaced by sadness. There was something else, too. If there's respect in death, that must be what I felt.

Silently, I stood, still looking at the buck. For some reason, I remembered that subzero evening the previous December. I had hollered something about the buck winning — until the next year.

I realized that killing the buck didn't mean I had won the game. Hunting isn't about winning or losing.

In my heart, where the only true scores are kept, he'll always be the winner.

What I Learned

It might sound redundant, but dedication and hard work are priceless when chasing mature whitetails. Often during my two-year pursuit of the buck, I almost gave up. However, I stuck with it.

I can't explain the energy I expended those two seasons. I spent dozens of hours and walked countless miles trying to determine how the buck was using his home area. Eventually, I knew where the buck fed, bedded and traveled.

After that, I merely had to show restraint to keep from burning out on the area.

A Monster Nontypical

The buck featured in the previous two chapters was unusual because I saw him several times during the two years I hunted him. The buck in this chapter is also unusual — for different reasons.

My brother Jeff and I chased this buck for two seasons, but we never saw him until one fateful day. We tracked him through rubs on 6- to 8-inch poplars, and during winter, we'd occasionally find his huge hoofprints. That combination eventually led me to a stand overlooking one of the buck's primary travel corridors.

However, I probably wouldn't have been there the afternoon of Dec. 13, 1990, if not for Jeff.

The Long Campaign

That season didn't start out well. In September, a good friend and I bow-hunted whitetails in Manitoba with mutual friend Randy Bean. However, as is typical when I bow-hunt Canada, the weather didn't cooperate. We endured high winds and warm temperatures, and deer movement was markedly suppressed.

Still, I almost killed a huge 10-point buck I'm sure would have made Boone and Crockett. He stood 15 yards away for almost five minutes, as I drooled over his rack. However, he was behind me, so I had to turn in my tree stand to shoot. I almost made it. I was at full draw and settling in for the shot when the buck suddenly turned and ran.

I attributed it to bad luck, but it seemed to be a premonition.

In late October and early November, I hunted with Jim Hole Jr. of Classic Outfitters Ltd. in Edmonton, Alberta — with similar results. Jim and his guide, Wolfgang Hoffmann, worked as hard as anyone I've seen to put me and Pennsylvanian Chris Green onto big bucks. Of course, the week after I left, action picked up, and Jim's hunters killed a half-dozen Pope and Young bucks.

Even a return trip to Manitoba during prime time in mid-November didn't work.

I saw many bucks, including so many P&Y-class deer that I lost count. One, a massive, dark-antlered buck that would have scored 140 to 150, ran to within 15 yards, stopped and provided a shot for which I had waited all fall. How I blew it remains a mystery.

Between my Canada jaunts, I chased whitetails in Wisconsin. Jeff and I focused on a farm about 30 miles from home, where we'd seen a huge deer and abundant big-buck sign. We thought the area might hold a Boone and Crockett buck.

During October, Jeff and I didn't see the big deer. In fact, we had trouble seeing average bucks. We had found many big rubs during the pre-rut the previous year, but they almost disappeared that fall. But because of the sign we'd found in previous seasons — and because the farm was so close to home — we continued to hunt it, hoping something would snap. However, it never happened — maybe because of that season's strange rut.

We experienced a highlight during the nine-day November gun season, when Jeff shot the largest buck of his career on the fourth morning. I was as happy about that big-bodied 10-pointer as Jeff. My "little" brother had been in on many hunts when other folks killed big bucks, but it was his turn. I enjoyed watching him affix his tag to a real trophy.

Immediately after gun season, I hunted in Georgia with Realtree camouflage designer Bill Jordan. I had a great time and saw many bucks — just no shooters. It seemed my bad luck was

The highlight of the gun season was when my brother Jeff shot a brute buck — the biggest he had killed — on the fourth morning.

I knew bucks were in a post-rut pattern, so the approaching snow and cold would trigger activity. I immediately made plans to hunt.

holding true. However, that's something every trophy hunter must learn to accept. Some seasons, nothing goes right.

Apparently, 1990 would be one of those years.

The Worm Turns

I hadn't thought about late-season bow-hunting after I returned from Georgia. Actually, I was catching up on writing assignments when Jeff stopped at my house Dec. 12. He had just returned from scouting the farm.

He asked whether I'd seen big rubs near the stand I hunted earlier that fall. I hadn't.

"Well, you've got a big deer or two working that area now," he said. "I saw at least three fresh rubs on 6- and 8-inch poplar trees within 75 yards of your stand. I know you've had a terrible year and probably don't feel like hunting any more, but don't give up. If you've got some spare time, I think it would be well worth it to sit in your stand for a few hours."

The stand was 14 feet high in a big oak on the edge of a huge alfalfa field. I had selected the oak the previous year because it was in range of two active rub lines that met at the intersection of a bluff and a brushy fence line. During 1990, however, I had only seen a couple of big rubs on either side, and the largest buck I had seen on stand was a half-racked 4-pointer. That was partly why I wasn't enthusiastic about the late season. Jeff's findings quickly changed my attitude, however.

The weather helped, too. It had been unseasonably warm the first week of December but had cooled considerably the second week. While listening to the forecast the afternoon Jeff stopped, I learned a major snowstorm was headed toward Wisconsin, followed by a trough of Arctic air. Bucks were in a post-rut pattern, so the approaching snow and cold would undoubtedly trigger activity.

I immediately made plans to hunt.

That Cold December Day

The next afternoon, a Thursday, I climbed into my stand and

replayed the events of Fall 1990. The distraction helped me forget the cold.

A slight wind blew that afternoon but stopped just before sunset. With no air moving, the temperature seemed to increase. I was confident I could sit until shooting hours expired.

Then, I heard a deer approaching from behind.

Three inches of snow had remained on the ground during the warm spell. With the recent cold snap, however, it had formed a noisy crust. I listened to the first deer approach for almost 30 seconds before I saw it — still 75 yards away. It was a buck fawn. If he stayed on the runway, he would walk under me.

I had no intention of shooting the little buck, and because no other deer followed him, I turned my back. In seconds, he was under me, and I heard him stop. I expected him to continue into the alfalfa field. However, he suddenly whirled and ran back from where he'd come. He stood 75 yards behind me for a couple of minutes, looking toward me. Suddenly, he issued a half-dozen loud snorts and ran out of sight.

"Well," I thought, "that ruins this stand for the afternoon. Every deer within earshot will know something is wrong."

I wasn't surprised. That was the way things had gone all fall.

The little buck's snorts had barely died when I heard other deer walking in the crunchy snow. I couldn't believe it, but they were headed for the field. Obviously, the button buck's ruckus wouldn't keep them from hitting the alfalfa.

The deer were walking through the wooded bluff to my left and would come out about 100 yards away. I shifted my attention to a wooded point that jutted into the field. Suddenly, deer started popping into the open. Three does emerged first, looked around, and then started feeding. I heard more deer coming, and then four more does slowly edged out of the woods. I was already standing, but because none of the deer had antlers, I didn't take my bow off the hanger.

Slowly putting my hands back in my pockets, I leaned against the oak and again concentrated on staying warm.

The big buck stood just 15 yards away for almost five minutes, letting me drool over his huge rack. However, he was behind me.

I knew the deer were walking through the wooded bluff to my left. Suddenly, they popped into the open.

There He Is

Eventually, the does fed to within 15 yards. Now and then, one stuck her nose into the air, sniffed for a few seconds and stamped her front foot. The other deer would get nervous, move off and look around. Then, however, they would relax and again start pawing through the snow at the alfalfa. I couldn't feel a breeze, but there must have been enough to swirl my scent around the field corner. Occasionally, one of the does caught a whiff and got worked up. Thankfully, I had showered and donned fresh clothes before the hunt.

Twenty minutes after the does appeared, I heard another deer walking through the woods along the bluff to my left. Instead of emerging where the does had, however, it stayed inside the woods until it was 50 yards away. Convinced it was another doe, I didn't bother looking when it walked into the field.

When I finally turned my head, I almost fell out of the tree.

One of the largest bucks I'd seen was walking toward me. He was already within 30 yards and closing. Instinctively, I grabbed for my bow with my left hand. The does beneath me immediately spooked and bolted. I held my breath and peeked at the buck. He had stopped, head erect and ears pinned back, looking at the retreating does.

"That's it," I thought. "He's going to run back into the woods."

But he dropped his head, flicked his tail and started toward me again. Slowly, I grabbed my bow and removed it from the hanger. The buck must have caught a hint of movement, because he stopped again and seemed to look up at me. I stood still, and after a 20-second staredown, the deer dropped his head and resumed approaching.

He was just 20 yards away. It seemed he would continue past me broadside at less than 15 yards — the shot every bow-hunter dreams of.

I lifted my bow, got my feet in shooting position and waited. Just as I was ready to draw, the buck suddenly turned head-on, stopped and started feeding. That wasn't part of the plan.

Having a huge buck 15 yards away with nothing between you is a true test of nerves. I considered shooting but quickly dismissed the idea. There was no way to ensure a fatal hit. I would wait till he turned broadside.

With more than 20 minutes of shooting time remaining, I knew the buck would eventually provide the angle I needed.

The Shot

After almost three minutes, the buck finally stepped to the right. I silently urged him to take another step and, as if heeding, he did — exposing his right side. I came to full draw, lined up the pin, made sure my sight picture was perfect and fired. The Zwickey-tipped shaft covered the 45 feet almost instantly. I thought the arrow hit exactly where I wanted, but the buck whirled and ran before I could tell.

At first, the buck headed for the bluff. After three or four bounds, though, he noticed the does running across the field. He turned slightly and fell in line with them. I stayed on my stand and watched as the buck ran to 100 yards. I thought I saw his butt sag slightly, but I couldn't be sure. When the deer reached 150 yards, I began to doubt my shot. When he passed 200 yards, I was concerned. Then, the does turned left. As the buck followed, he suddenly piled up. He was down!

The excitement was almost too much to bear. I waited several minutes to collect my thoughts, watching the fallen buck. When it was apparent he wouldn't get up, I climbed down.

I likely covered the 200-plus yards to the deer in world-class time. As I approached, it became obvious the antlers were wider and more massive than they had initially appeared.

Further, the rack had more points. At first, I had thought the deer was a basic 10-pointer with a couple of stickers. He was far better. A preliminary tally counted 17 points, with two stickers on his bases that were almost of scorable length (1 inch). After counting the points again, I placed the giant deer's head back in the snow and sat next to him. For five minutes, I simply admired him. My feelings were indescribable.

Although it was extremely difficult, I left the buck in the field and walked to find help. Later, I met Jeff and his friend Brian Crane at the landowner's house, and we drove to retrieve my deer. On the way out, I stopped to show the landowner and then left for home.

The buck field dressed at 190 pounds. Obviously, he had been active during the rut, because he didn't have a speck of fat. He was so skinny that his backbone and hip bones stuck out like those of an underfed horse. I've never killed a deer in such poor condition. My taxidermist later said the measurements from the buck's cape were consistent with those of a 230- to 240-pound animal. A preliminary check of the deer's teeth indicated he was at least $7^{1}/_{2}$.

The buck's rack had a symmetrical 10-point frame with eight

additional abnormal points. The main beam lengths were 27⁶/₈ and 26³/₈ inches. The brow tines measured 10 and 9¹/₈ inches, and the next-longest tines were 9¹/₈ and 7⁴/₈ inches. Five of the eight circumference measurements were more than 5 inches, and the smallest was 4⁶/₈. The bases measured 5³/₈ and 6²/₈. The outside spread was almost 24 inches, and the inside spread was 21¹/₈. The gross nontypical score was at 202⁵/₈.

Conclusion

I hadn't seen that buck till minutes before I shot him. Still, I had never doubted I was hunting a large deer. The buck had consistently rubbed 6- to 8-inch trees the two years I had tracked him. Further, Jeff and I had continually found huge hoofprints on the property.

As is common with big bucks, that nontypical had maintained a low profile. The evening of Dec. 13, 1990, however, the desire to eat had outweighed his normal caution. I was just in the right place at the right time.

I guess 1990 wasn't such a bad year after all.

Showdown at High Noon

In November 1992, I returned to Alberta for another gun hunt. It was memorable, but not just because of all the big bucks I saw. The trip also produced valuable, treasured friendships.

However, another element made the hunt more memorable. I've never expended so much effort to kill a big buck. My outfitter and guide, Terry Birkholz, is as dedicated and serious about hunting mature whitetails as anyone I've met. I didn't know anyone was as willing to walk the extra miles or sit the extra hours required to kill mature deer.

From the start, I knew the hunt would be special.

An Awesome Beginning

The bucks in the poplar thicket sounded dandy. Large branches snapped like dried kindling as the combatants tried to intimidate each other. Occasionally, heavy footfalls of posturing bucks echoed forth. No doubt, the sound carried a long way in the early-morning calm.

Abruptly, the brush busting and branch breaking ended, and a deep grunt echoed through the stillness. Seconds later, I heard antlers aggressively raking a tree. This disturbance continued for about 15 seconds, followed by silence. The stillness was then shattered by violent crashing and grinding antlers.

From 60 yards away, I envisioned two bull-shouldered Alberta bucks trying to assert their dominance on each other. But that wasn't the case. The fight was staged.

Although stand hunting remains the most effective strategy, it isn't the only option. My guide and outfitter, Terry Birkholz, has been successful with still-hunting and rattling.

Terry was buried in a poplar thicket, trying to imitate two bucks having a knock-down, drag-out battle. I was slightly in front of him, with a decent field of fire for several directions. I soon learned I had chosen my location perfectly.

Terry had just started the first sequence when I heard an answering grunt. At first, I thought it had come from thick brush in front of me. However, a second grunt convinced me the buck was slightly behind me and to my left. About 40 yards in that direction, a four-strand barbwire fence paralleled a railroad grade. The brush in which I was hidden stopped about 10 yards on my side of the fence line. The 10 yards of open ground was covered with waist-high yellow grass, which was covered with thick hoarfrost.

As I strained to see the buck, a dark, heavy, long-tined rack appeared. Apparently, the buck was in a slight swale in the tall grass and was heading past me at an easy lope. I watched in amazement as the buck coasted past at 20 yards. He continued by and stopped in the open about 60 yards away, listening and looking for the fight, and giving me a chance to analyze his rack.

The buck's right antler was long-beamed and heavy, with a 6-inch brow tine and extremely long G-2 and G-3 tines. His G-4 was only about 2 inches. However, the left side of his rack stopped me from shooting. It had a 6-inch brow tine and a 10- to 12-inch G-2 — and that was it! His stubbed-out left main beam was probably no longer than 18 inches. The buck was a typical 5-by-3, with an inside spread of almost 22 inches. If his left side had matched his right, he likely would have gross-scored almost 160. The buck was a unique trophy — just not the type of deer for which I had traveled to Alberta.

That was the second day of a six-day trip with Terry. He and his partner, Dave Bzawy, own Alberta Wilderness Guide Service and operate two camps. Terry's camp is almost three hours south and east of Edmonton, near the small town of Edgerton. The area is mostly cultivated farmland, and wheat is the main crop. Dave's base is near Smokey Lake, about an hour north and slightly east of Edmonton. It features larger stands of uncleared aspen but enough farmland to provide whitetails with excellent nutrition.

The camps have similar success rates, mostly because Dave and Terry are so familiar with the areas. Also, they spend lots of time studying and patterning bucks.

Hunters at the camps sit on stands in peak buck-activity areas. That, plus a strict no-road-hunting policy, attracted me to the operation.

However, as illustrated in the previous hunt, stand-hunting isn't the only option. Terry and Dave have learned that rattling and still-hunting also work. They've experienced success with those tactics because they have a thorough understanding of mature bucks and tremendous familiarity with their hunting areas.

I had killed a 150-class buck during a 1986 Alberta gun-hunt with Russell Thornberry. Since then, I had wanted to return for another go at a big deer. I was excited when Terry confirmed my booking for Nov. 15 through 21.

Close Calls

The first day held plenty of excitement. In just more than an hour, I had two 170-class bucks in my cross hairs. However, because of their amazing survival abilities, I couldn't shoot at either.

The first buck caught Terry and me flat-footed. We were walking across a wheat field, trying to detour around a 1½-year-old buck, when a black-horned monster loped over a steep hill 75 yards away. We saw the buck simultaneously. I knew immediately that the deer was a shooter, and so I shouldered my .300 Win. Mag. Before I could get a decent sight picture, however, the deer whirled and sped back over the hill. I sprinted to the crest, but he was gone.

A quick analysis with Terry confirmed my suspicions. Although the deer had been visible for just seconds, we knew I had missed a heck of a chance. He was a heavy, long-tined 10-pointer with several sticker points. Terry figured the buck would gross-score more than 170. As I soon learned, however, the excitement hadn't ended.

Less than an hour later, I had another big buck in my sights. That

During the first three and a half days of my hunt, I had seen super bucks. However, I didn't have anything to show for my efforts.

Terry managed to rattle in a 140-class 8-pointer. The buck was so close, I'm sure I could have hit it in the face with a handful of sand.

deer crossed a power line about 200 yards away. He kept his head down in low brush in the power cut, and although I occasionally glimpsed long tines, I couldn't see enough to warrant shooting.

Terry later said the buck had run across a huge wheat field before reaching the power line. He was sure the long-tined buck would have grossed more than 170 inches.

What a way to start a hunt.

Walking and Rattling

The third day, I watched a secluded power line for almost four hours. I rattled periodically throughout the morning, and attracted a small buck, a doe and fawn, and a coyote. Terry arrived at about 11 a.m. with a couple of sandwiches and a thermos of coffee. As I ate, he discussed a new game plan.

"This is really a huge area of cover," he said, unfolding an aerial photo. "I think we should spend a couple of hours walking and rattling in likely looking spots. The wind is blowing hard enough to ensure that we can move from one area to another without creating too much of a disturbance."

I agreed.

We spent the rest of the day walking and rattling. We jumped a tremendous buck that was bedded with a doe, and rattled in a 140-class 4-by-4. The 8-pointer was so close I probably could have hit him with a handful of sand. His rack was fairly heavy, featuring good tine length and an inside spread of about 20 inches. His antler bases and skull cap were covered with green shredded bark. It was an unforgettable sight.

The next morning, Terry took me to a new area and set me up at a long power-cut line.

"There are some wheat fields off in the distance," he said. "The deer you see this morning will probably be making their way back from those fields."

Before he walked into the pre-dawn darkness, he told me hunters had killed some tremendous deer in that area.

That morning, I saw two does, three fawns and two huge bucks.

One of the bucks was a wide-antlered brute I saw as he walked down the cut line 500 yards away. The other was a huge nontypical that would have surpassed 200 inches. He stepped into the power line 200 yards to my right and walked straight away. I slid off the padded stool, rested the rifle atop the stool and followed the buck in my scope.

I feel confident shooting my McMillan-stocked Ruger at that range, especially with a solid rest. I waited for the buck to turn and quarter away slightly, which he did at 250 yards. I put slight pressure on the trigger, and the rifle roared.

Immediately, I knew I had cleanly missed the deer. A subsequent examination proved it. What can I say?

As you might imagine, I was depressed. I had seen five super bucks and had legitimate chances at three, yet I had nothing to show. Still, I didn't give up, so when Terry asked if I wanted to try rattling or return to camp early for a photo shoot, I opted for the former.

About an hour later, the rattling session ended without attracting a deer. When we reached the truck, Terry glanced at his watch.

"We've got about a half-hour before we're supposed to be back at camp," he said. "Should we head back now or try rattling in one more spot?"

Again, I suggested rattling.

Terry pinpointed our next rattling location via aerial photo. It took us almost 20 minutes to sneak into the spot, but almost immediately, my confidence soared. Fresh buck sign was everywhere. Also, we found where two bucks had battled atop a slight rise. Terry pointed to several scuff marks on the ground and gave me a silent thumbs-up.

We continued for 75 yards and then split up. Terry sneaked down into a wooded draw, and I set up 50 yards to one side and slightly in front of him, atop a small rise covered with forearm-sized poplars. I knelt and peered into the thick cover. Any buck responding to rattling would likely sneak in from that direction.

Just before Terry started his first rattling sequence, I heard a large

The look on Terry's face said it all. After meeting frustration at every turn, we finally managed to do everything right. It was a special moment.

deer to my right suddenly burst from its bed and crash away. Several times, I heard antlers hitting branches as the unseen buck continued, circling slightly in front of me. There was no way the deer winded me, but he obviously reacted to a noise he couldn't identify.

I listened and watched as Terry rattled. The only response came from a doe that snorted and blew steadily somewhere behind him. We waited and watched for 10 minutes before Terry started his second sequence. The smashing, raking, grunting and rattling continued for several minutes, and then all was quiet again. Nothing.

We had been at the spot for almost 25 minutes when Terry rattled again. No more than 15 seconds later, I saw him suddenly drop his antlers and dive behind a tree. He noticed I was looking at him and quickly yet subtly pointed over his shoulder. I assumed he had seen a deer approaching from that direction, but I couldn't see a thing.

That was nerve-racking. The deer could have been a good buck, yet for almost a minute, I couldn't detect movement. Then suddenly, I glimpsed a deer moving through a small opening. Before I could identify it, however, it stepped behind a large poplar. At least I knew where the deer was.

The deer flicked its tail and then drifted through another opening into a slight draw. Just before it disappeared, I glimpsed antlers. However, I still hadn't seen enough to know how big he was.

A rise was in front of the buck, and the only cover was knee-high yellow grass. After about a minute, the buck walked out of the draw and onto the open rise, and then turned broadside, giving me a great view of his rack.

He was one of the largest typical whitetails I've seen. However, although the buck was in the open, I couldn't shoot. The rise on which I sat was covered with thick brush. No matter how much I strained my eyes or moved my head, I couldn't find an opening to slip a bullet through.

The big buck had walked within 25 yards of Terry and stood atop the rise, staring hard into the draw. I knew the deer would soon know it had been duped, so I had to act quickly. Leaning back as far as I could, I found a small, 1-square-foot opening. I shouldered my rifle and leveled the cross hairs on the buck's left shoulder. Just before I shot, I noticed the buck had turned his head and was looking at me. The bullet was already on its way.

At the hit, the buck kicked his hind legs and took off on a full-speed, head-down charge. Unfortunately, he chose the rise on which I stood as his escape route. Believe me, you don't know fear until you've seen a hog-bodied, huge-racked Alberta whitetail bearing down on you. Not knowing what else to do, I stood and quickly chambered a fresh round into the .300.

At 20 feet, the buck suddenly turned slightly and crashed past, seemingly within arm's reach. Although I felt confident about the initial hit, I slammed two more point-blank shots at the buck as he motored by.

And that quickly, he disappeared.

I listened as he ran over dead branches and underbrush, and then everything was quiet. For some reason, I glanced at my watch. It was noon.

Quickly, Terry was next to me.

"I want you to know that was a really big buck," he said excitedly. "Did you make a good hit?"

I assured him that the first shot should have been on the money. As we talked, I reloaded my rifle. Then, we took a few more steps to where the buck had run past me. There was abundant blood, so we trailed the deer immediately. We found the buck after 150 yards.

It was a thrill walking up on the monster deer. His huge body and tremendous antler height provided an impressive sight. Terry and I shook hands and slapped each other on the back. Then, we became relatively quiet and simply admired the majestic deer.

The rack was a basic 10-pointer with three stickers, including a 4-inch muley-like point off the left G-2. The inside spread was $17^4/_8$ inches, and each main beam was longer than 27 inches. The G-2s measured $14^1/_8$ and $11^3/_8$, and the G-3s were $9^3/_8$ and $8^6/_8$. The base circumference measurements were $5^1/_8$ and 5, and the smallest cir-

After taking a few photos at the kill site, we dragged my buck to a nearby wheat field and snapped some more pictures.

cumference was 4²/₈. Amazingly, the rack sported short brow tines, which measured a mere 2⁴/₈ and 2⁶/₈. Still, the buck gross-scored slightly more than 180 typical inches. He would probably net in the low 170s.

That's a very good deer, even by Canadian standards.

What I Learned

It was a great hunt. However, as usual, it's difficult to describe the effort expended. Like most of the other mature deer I've killed, that buck was shot only after hard work and dedication.

I can't lie, however. It was difficult not to get frustrated after having several close calls with big bucks the first three days of the hunt. However, I believed that every lost opportunity only put me closer to when everything would come together.

Perhaps the most valuable lesson was that it takes a special blend of factors to create a memorable hunt. Of course, killing a huge whitetail is one. However, the bond Terry and I developed during my stay was equally important. My memories wouldn't have been as special if not for Terry. It's not often you can spend time with someone who's as dedicated and serious about trophy whitetail hunting as you. It's a privilege to call Terry my friend.

A Two-Year Quest Ends

I don't consider myself a deer hunting expert. I think "deer hunting educator" more accurately describes what I do. The three books and hundreds of magazine articles I've written, plus my many seminars, are designed to inform hunters about killing mature bucks. I try to help folks realize their dreams by killing a bragging-sized whitetail.

Regardless of the topic, I always discuss several critical points, the most important of which is expectations.

Many up-and-coming trophy hunters think success will come quickly. However, success with big bucks doesn't occur overnight. The previous chapters of this book have highlighted some of my most memorable deer hunts. Many involved deer killed in different locales through many years. However, one element has remained constant: Success didn't come easily or quickly. A couple of the hunts spanned two seasons!

Recently, I've noticed a disturbing trend with young trophy hunters. They seek — and expect — instant gratification. Further, they don't want to hunt a big buck hard for weeks, months or years.

I'm not making this up. During the past few years, many young hunters have told me they "don't have time to waste" chasing big bucks. They want me to tell them how to find, pattern and kill a big buck as quickly as possible — preferably within days. When I tell them that's impossible, they're skeptical.

"I'm willing to bet you have a secret for figuring out big bucks that you're not sharing with the rest of us," a young hunter said recently.

I've noticed a disturbing trend with younger trophy hunters. Too many expect instant gratification.

I assume he was referring to some shortcut.

Sure, I enter each hunt with optimism. However, I constantly remind myself that it might not happen that day. I've learned that keeping that mindset provides a good balance. I expect to get a chance at a big buck every hunt, but I can also handle disappointment if that doesn't occur.

I've mentioned that for a reason. During November 1998, I killed a great buck in Iowa. The hunt culminated from two years of hard work by me and my good friend Joe Loomis. Joe and I had discovered the buck a year before we began hunting him. We knew almost everything about the buck, including where he ate, drank, bedded and rutted.

However, we just couldn't determine his travel patterns.

The Buck Shows Up

Sometime in February 1997, I received a packet of photos from Joe. He had placed a motion-detection camera near a cornfield on his property. Deep snow and brutally cold weather had deer piling into Joe's farm to feed, and the resulting photos were unbelievable.

One of the bucks was familiar. Joe had been watching the monster 10-pointer since buying the farm two years earlier. The buck had been mature then, and Joe figured the deer was at least 6½ when it was photographed.

"I found this buck's sheds last spring," Joe wrote on one of the photos. "Based on the measurements of those antlers and how much he's grown since, I'd say the buck would probably gross score close to 190 typical."

Several other mature bucks were pictured, and one caught my eye. He sported a beautiful 10-point rack. I was impressed with the width and symmetry of the antlers and the incredible body size of the deer.

"That's a heck of a buck," I thought.

I received another packet of photos from Joe two months later. Obviously, the deer had become accustomed to the camera. Also, the larger bucks had apparently relaxed their guard somewhat. Most of the pictures from the first packet had been taken after dark. However, at least half the photos from the second packet were shot during daylight — including numerous pictures of the Boone and Crockett buck and the wide 10-pointer.

Close Call for the 10

Because of a schedule conflict, I couldn't bow-hunt Iowa during November 1997. However, Joe suggested I set aside a week in December to hunt the late archery season.

"I plan on leaving some of my corn standing all winter," he said. "There should be lots of deer on my property by the end of the month. And the worse the weather gets, the better the hunting will be."

That sounded good.

Meanwhile, Joe let a couple of other bow-hunters on his property during the rut, and one almost killed the wide 10-pointer. It was about during the second week of November when the buck temporarily abandoned caution.

A hot doe had cruised by the hunter. Minutes later, the guy heard a

Joe said this big buck would probably gross-score almost 190 typical.

deer running through a deep valley below his stand. Suddenly, a wide-racked 10-pointer charged into view. The hunter became rattled, and instead of shooting the deer through the vitals, he hit the buck square in the shoulder blade. The shaft penetrated just 2 inches.

Joe told me about the incident two weeks later.

"Don't worry, Greg," he said. "The buck is still alive. I've seen him a couple of times this past week. He's also walked by my camera a few times, so I got some more photos of him. He's got a small scar on his shoulder, but other than that, he's OK."

No Luck in December

I planned to leave Wisconsin Dec. 26 for my late-season Iowa hunt. My son, Jake, had several days off from school, so I asked if he would like to accompany me. He was all for it. Eight hours after leaving home, we pulled into Joe's driveway. It was snowing and very cold. I couldn't have asked for better conditions.

The buck on the left is the wide 10-pointer I was hunting. The buck on the right is the nontypical that appeared in 1998.

I was only vaguely familiar with the property, so I decided to not hunt the first morning. I didn't want to stumble around in the pre-dawn darkness and alert deer that something was up. Instead, I waited till midmorning, when Joe showed me some hotspots. As I learned, however, it was pretty much wasted effort.

I decided to set up in a bottleneck atop a narrow ridge. According to Joe, a couple of big bucks routinely bedded in a deep, thick valley west of the ridge. Most afternoons, the bucks would travel to the top of the narrow ridge and follow it to a distant clover field. If they stuck with that routine, they would pass within 15 yards of my stand.

I'd only been on stand about a half-hour when I suddenly felt ill. The feeling only lasted about a minute. Fifteen minutes later, however, I felt ill again. A wave of nausea hit me, and I began sweating. I leaned my head back against the tree and closed my eyes, but that only brought on dizziness. Frustrated and confused, I lowered my bow and climbed down.

I thought I had some type of 24-hour flu. However, I didn't feel better the next morning. Actually, I felt worse. I stayed inside all day, hoping to snap out of it by afternoon. But I didn't.

I stuck it out another two days but made it to the woods only once. At daylight the next morning, Jake and I were packed and ready to head home. A trip to the local clinic revealed that I had a bad sinus infection. Strong antibiotics had me rarin' to go after a week, but hunting season was finished.

Photos and a Rut-Hunt

Thanks to Joe and his spy camera, we kept tabs on the big bucks. The most interesting photos were of velvet-antlered monsters in late Summer 1998. The wide 10-pointer and the old monarch appeared frequently. We also had several photos of a large nontypical. Hopefully, the bucks would stick around during the rut.

I planned to hunt Iowa with Joe and Jake the first week of November. It was raining hard when we pulled into his yard the night of Halloween 1998. Further, the forecast called for more of the same the next two days. Undaunted, Jake and I spent the first morning scouting and placing stands. With the number of big bucks on the property, I figured it was just a matter of time before one gave us a chance — rain or no rain.

One small, lush clover field Joe had shown us really piqued my interest. It was unique because it was surrounded by woods.

"This would be a great place for a decoy setup," I said to Jake. "Let's go ahead and put up a stand."

It didn't take long for Jake to see action. The first afternoon, a large 10-pointer with a long sticker point off his G-2 approached the decoy. The buck approached to 40 yards and was closing rapidly when the unthinkable happened: The decoy suddenly tipped over. (That happened frequently during the hunt because of high winds and saturated ground.)

Jake later said the buck had simply stopped and stared at the fallen decoy. Seconds later, he resumed walking toward the decoy.

"I put Jake in a stand near the edge of a small clover field. I then placed a buck decoy 20 yards away. He saw action almost immediately."

Here's a much better look at the wide 10-pointer that continually wandered in front of Joe's camera.

However, he became suspicious just before coming within range, so he circled to the far side of the decoy — out of range.

The deer stood and stared at the fallen decoy for almost five minutes before turning and casually walking away. Amazingly, he wasn't alarmed. I told Jake the buck might return another day.

I had positioned Jake's stand so he could walk out of the area without spooking deer. Further, it was in a spot that let him take advantage of the prevailing winds. During our trip, no deer winded him.

Typically, I wouldn't have let Jake hunt the same spot every day. However, based on his experience the first two days, deer hadn't detected him. He was seeing does, fawns, small bucks, large bucks and even huge bucks in and near the clover field. We believed it was only a matter of time before another buck checked out the decoy. He begged me to let him continue hunting his hotspot, and I couldn't disagree.

Meanwhile, I tried to stay out of Jake's way and find one of the farm's big bucks. I'd waited near a buck crossing but had seen nothing. I'd also sat on a stand overlooking a parallel runway but had seen nothing. Out of desperation, I'd even placed a stand in a huge cottonwood in the middle of a cornfield. To add allure, I placed a buck decoy 20 yards from the base of the tree.

Sunset was still an hour away when I began a rattling sequence. I barely had time to hang up the antlers when I heard a deer crashing through a brushy draw about 200 yards behind me. Moments later, I saw a rack floating toward me above some tall yellow grass. It looked like a shooter buck.

I grabbed my bow and turned until I was facing the decoy. As is typical, the buck emerged, saw the bogus deer and immediately bristled. Instantly, he began walking stiff-legged toward the decoy. As the buck passed under me, I viewed his rack and realized he wasn't a shooter.

The buck, which I judged to be an exceptional $2^1/_2$-year-old, was a basic 9-pointer. His rack was tall and fairly wide, but it lacked the mass of a more mature whitetail. Still, I wished Jake would have been standing in the cottonwood. The 125-class deer would

Joe Loomis poses with the monarch that roamed his property for many years. The buck had to be at least 8½. What a trophy!

have been a great bow-kill for him.

The 10-Pointer Appears

That was my only highlight during the first five days. Thankfully, Jake continued to see bucks, so he was happy. That made the trip worthwhile.

During the last morning of our hunt, I decided to try the parallel-runway stand again. I hadn't seen much there, but something had seemed right. That's difficult to explain unless you've experienced it.

As I stepped onto my stand, I heard a deer walking through frozen oak leaves to my left. It was already daylight, so I easily saw the deer. It was a big buck! I quickly pulled up my bow, untied the tow rope and nocked an arrow. The buck had closed within 50 yards.

I looked again and almost fell out of the tree: It was the wide 10-pointer I'd seen in the photos!

The big whitetail continued toward me as if on a string. He stopped briefly to scan the woods, and then plodded on in a characteristic rut-walk. I waited until he was broadside at 25 yards and grunted with my voice. He skidded to a halt. The sight pin locked on, and I touched the release.

The mounted head of that 150-class buck — which had sprouted an 11th point — now hangs in my living room.

What I Learned

Again, I learned that work and dedication are priceless. I also learned that when hunting mature whitetails, the situation can change from really bad to very good in seconds. Finally, I learned that, sometimes, you should hunt a stand because something about it seems right.

Incidentally, a week and a half after returning from Iowa, I received a call from Joe. He had arrowed the huge old buck that had roamed his property for so many years. The majestic rack reflected the buck's age. He had lost much of the incredible tine length from the previous year, and the rack was considerably narrower. However, the rack made up for that in mass. The buck's main beams were palmated and extremely heavy. Any trophy hunter would have been proud of such a deer.

I know Joe was.

It seemed fitting that the old monarch had fallen to an arrow launched by the man who had chased him for almost four seasons.

A Big One for Jake

I've always had a great relationship with my son, Jake. I'm sure that's because I've spent lots of time with him.

When Jake was born, I was a seasonal construction worker for a concrete contractor. If you've spent much time in Wisconsin, you know it's almost impossible to pave roads and pour sidewalks, curbs and gutters during winter. Basically, I worked from April until some time in November and was laid off the rest of the year.

Jake was my constant companion during winter and went everywhere with me. I took him spring scouting when he was only 2. Several times, I let him ride on my back when we left the woods — a small price considering how much I enjoyed his company.

Jake's History

I remember one late-January day when Jake was 4. I'd received an assignment for a magazine article about post-season scouting, and it called for photos of "well-traveled winter runways." I knew the perfect place. As usual, Jake wanted to go along, and as I usually did, I agreed.

We were about to walk out the door when Jake suddenly turned and ran into the living room. I heard him digging in his toy box, and he soon ran back holding something..

"I wanted to bring this along, Dad," he said, holding aloft a toy camera. "I want to take some pictures too."

Jake found his first shed when he was 6. The 3-point antler was small, no doubt dropped by a 1½-year-old buck. However, that

I'd scouted the area and found a great place to put Jake during the gun-hunt opener.

didn't matter to Jake. He considered it a prize, and I guess I did, too. Watching him pick up that shed was special.

Jake first spent time in a tree stand when he was 8. I had received a bear permit that year, and Jake wanted to join me. He helped me run baits for a month before the season and put up tree stands opening day.

I'm proud to say that Jake saw the first bear. We had been on our stands for about an hour when he nudged me in the ribs. I turned my head and noticed Jake pointing to our left. I followed his gaze and was surprised to see a bear standing 20 yards away. The bruin eventually eased toward us and walked under our stands toward the bait. I was seeking a larger bear, so I passed the shot. Jake later bragged to his school buddies that he had been within 15 feet of a wild bear. I had to tell his teacher that he was telling the truth.

During the next three years, Jake accompanied me on hunts for foxes, coyotes, turkeys and deer, and he was always eager to join me on scouting trips and shed-antler excursions. He seemed to have a genuine interest in hunting, but I wondered — like any hunting parent — whether he would hunt deer when he turned 12.

Any doubts were erased when Jake turned 10. He didn't talk about hunting nonstop, but he mentioned it frequently. Also, his questions indicated he wanted to learn more about whitetails. I couldn't wait.

The next two years seemed to pass quickly. Before I knew it, I bought Jake his first hunting bow. Initially, I didn't think he would become proficient enough to start hunting. Eventually, though, his arrows began consistently hitting their mark. We were chomping at the bit for archery season.

We chased whitetails every available minute of the 1996 bow season and hunted hard during the nine-day gun season. Jake saw plenty of deer, including a Boone and Crockett-class buck. However, I never positioned his stand in the correct spot. Throughout fall, Jake remained upbeat and gung-ho. He was eager for the next season.

Before continuing, let me explain something. Before Jake's first season, I had been a dyed-in-the-wool big-woods hunter. At some point, however, I gave up the big woods. I could cite several reasons why, but let's just say the big woods didn't seem quite big enough anymore. It was time to move on.

Life Without the Big Woods

The transition from big woods to farmland went well. No doubt, it was smoother because Jake was my partner. I thought my departure from the big woods couldn't have happened at a better time. At Jake's age, he equated the quality of a hunt to how many deer he saw. And as I had painfully learned, deer sightings can be minimal in the big woods — even for experienced hunters. We wouldn't have that trouble in farmland. Deer numbers were at all-time highs, and Jake would have a ball.

I became so obsessed with helping Jake develop his hunting skills that my first year away from the big woods slipped by seamlessly. However, something happened that made those old feelings resurface. Jake and I were returning from a farmland bow-hunt when he became curious about my big-woods hunts. We talked for a while, and then he asked, "Do you think I'll ever get to hunt deer in the big woods, Dad?"

Something in Jake's voice told me that was more of a request.

We discussed big-woods deer hunting fairly often afterward. Each time, I told Jake about the negatives of chasing wilderness whitetails; about sometimes going days without seeing a deer, and that being successful would require working harder than ever before. He seemed undaunted, so I started planning a return to the North Woods.

Jake's second season was better. He made a great shot on a doe during a mid-October bow-hunt. About a month later, he killed his first buck during the fourth afternoon of gun season. The big-woods 5-pointer — much of its right antler had broken off — appeared an hour before dark, browsing on tender dogwood ends. I told Jake I'd grunt when the buck stepped into a small clearing, and he should shoot when the buck stopped. Everything worked, and I watched Jake make a great shot. The buck ran about 30 yards before dying.

Jake and I Find a Big Buck

During mid-September 1998, Jake, then 14, and I were pre-season scouting for the archery opener when we discovered a fresh rub line from a big buck. It ran between a major bedding area in a distant tamarack swamp and a nearby watering hole. It was pretty obvious, really. Wisconsin was enduring one of its hottest, driest years, and Jake and I were tromping through areas that were typically knee-deep in water. That fall, however, the ground was hard and dusty.

The big-woods area we were scouting was more than 20 miles in circumference without a through road. However, despite all the acreage, the buck apparently stayed in a relatively small area. Why not? The deer had everything he needed there, including food, water, cover and scores of antlerless deer. He wasn't going anywhere.

I sat next to Jake when he shot his first buck. The big-woods 5-pointer made it only 30 yards before piling up.

If we acted carefully, I thought, we could hunt the buck effectively through archery season. Even if we didn't ambush him then, we could hunt him during the nine-day gun season.

And I knew just where to place Jake's stand.

Close, But Not Quite

Twice during the early 1998 bow season, I thought Jake would kill the big buck. I had positioned his stand in the only tree near the water hole. Considering the weather, I figured the buck would quench his thirst daily. Jake's report from opening morning confirmed that. He had seen 14 deer, including two large bucks.

"Every one of the deer went right to the water hole to get a drink," he said. "Then they walked straight toward that big swamp behind my stand. None of the deer ever got any closer than 50 yards."

The second weekend of archery season provided more excitement. We were driving through the pre-dawn darkness several hundred yards from our hunting area when a giant buck ran across the road in front of us. I thought Jake would hyperventilate.

"Wow, did you see the size of that buck's rack?" he said. "He was at least a 10-pointer! Maybe he'll walk by one of us this morning."

Though I shared my son's excitement, I didn't share his optimism. However, I didn't know how prophetic his wish would be.

I had been on stand just 20 minutes that morning when a big buck appeared. One look confirmed that it was the deer Jake and I had seen run across the road. It also confirmed something else. If the big-woods deer stayed on course, he would walk within 15 yards of me. I grabbed my bow and got ready. The buck cut the distance to about 25 yards but, for no apparent reason, suddenly became wary. He stood still for almost five minutes, sniffing the air and studying his surroundings. Then, he turned and walked away.

I swear he simply sensed my presence.

As I learned later, the buck raised Jake's heart rate by several beats that morning. Jake was sitting on his stand when he noticed movement to his right. Turning his head, he was stunned to see three big bucks walking together. Judging from Jake's description, one was the same deer I'd seen earlier. Apparently, he'd picked up two traveling companions along the way.

The deer stayed out of range as they headed toward their bedding area. Still, Jake's sighting put several more pieces of the puzzle in place.

Jake and I continued bow-hunting the big-woods area through the first weeks of October. We saw many antlerless deer and small bucks, but the larger bucks seemed to go underground.

A business commitment prevented me from hunting during late October, and then Jake and I hunted Iowa deer for eight days in November. When we returned to Wisconsin, archery season had closed. However, as I had told Jake, there was always gun season.

Based on what we had learned, I was confident.

The big buck had picked up two traveling companions between my stand and Jake's.

Jake Gets His Chance

A couple of days before gun season, I relocated Jake's stand to a lone tamarack amid a narrow, fairly long grass marsh. During a scouting trip, I learned that one of the buck's rub lines ran past the tree and continued toward a narrow strip of high ground. I figured the buck was bedding there. If so, Jake would be in position to intercept him as he moved between bedding and feeding areas. However, as is often true, it was a gamble whether the deer would move in daylight during gun season.

Opening morning dawned cold and snowy. I saw seven antlerless deer and two small bucks, and Jake saw a doe and two fawns. At 10 a.m., we returned to camp to warm up, dry our clothes and get some much-needed brunch. We returned to our stands at about 1:30 p.m. Just before separating, I warned Jake to be especially alert.

"Make sure you keep an eye out toward that strip of high

ground to your left," I said. "The deer are going to be active after this snowfall. I wouldn't doubt you'll see something come out of that bedding area this afternoon."

Jake had been on stand two hours when he heard a loud grunt over his left shoulder. He turned and almost lost his breath. A monster buck was standing in the grassy marsh just 80 yards away!

Jake slowly brought up his .270 and centered the deer in the scope.

"But I couldn't keep the cross hairs on him, so I didn't shoot," he said later. "The next thing I knew, the buck had walked into some thick tag alders. I kept waiting for him to come back out in the open, but he didn't. Then, I heard him grunt a couple of times. It sounded like he was getting closer. He grunted again, and I could tell for sure he was coming my way. I got ready just in case.

"A few seconds later, I spotted the buck walking through the thick tag alders. He was headed straight for a small opening. I lined up the scope on the opening, and when I saw the cross hairs on his front shoulder, I squeezed the trigger. The buck kicked out his hind legs and ran out of the tag alder brush and into a stand of poplar trees."

Sharing Success

Ironically, I was also waiting for a big buck to clear thick brush near my stand when I heard Jake shoot. I forgot about that deer before the echoes faded. In seconds, I was on the ground and running toward Jake's stand. I quickly reached his tree and asked what happened. He briefed me and pointed to where the buck had been standing when he shot.

I immediately found the deer's trail in the snow — along with the start of a blood trail.

"By the look of things, this deer isn't going far," I said quietly "Climb down, Jake, and we'll track him together."

The trail led us through tag alders and into the poplars — right where Jake had last seen the buck. We had walked about 20 yards when I saw the buck on the ground ahead. The 130-grain bullet had done its job.

I stepped back and let Jake walk to the buck first. We spent 10 minutes high-fiving, hugging, laughing and silently admiring the great animal. The stout-bodied, massive-beamed 10-pointer exemplified what a swamp-loving, big-woods whitetail should look like.

"Enjoy this moment to the fullest, Jake," I said. "It might be a while before you find yourself in this position again."

My wife, Geralyn, and daughter, Jessie, were waiting at camp. Their faces lit up when Jake burst through the door.

"Come on, you two, get your boots on," he said. "You have to help us get my buck out of the woods."

Geralyn later said she could tell Jake wasn't joking. It took her and Jessie just minutes to don their boots and jackets.

Having our family participate in retrieving Jake's buck made it more special. However, I think the process — from when Jake and I found the deer in September till the fateful November day — was destined to play out that way.

Conclusion

Seeing Jake smile for the first time, hearing his first words, watching him take his first steps, helping him ride a bike and listening to tales of his first day at school were significant, memorable experiences.

That deer hunt ranks right up there.

Parents who hunt know what I mean. I understand the lump in your throats and the tears in your eyes when you recall similar moments with your sons or daughters. They are beyond description but live in our hearts and minds forever.

Since Jake was born, I dreamed of when he would join me as a hunter. Of course, I also dreamed about when he would shoot his first big buck. That day has come and gone, but the memories burn brightly.

I sure learned some things during Jake's hunt, but the most

Jake should be proud of his big 10-pointer. He logged many hours on stand waiting for the big whitetail to appear.

important lesson doesn't deal with tactics or strategies. It's about what makes a hunt special.

I've been blessed to kill some great whitetails and several trophy bears. Further, I still cherish a bull elk that charged in to investigate some cow-calling during an Oregon bow-hunt a couple of years ago.

However, none of those experiences were as important or memorable as Jake's 1998 big-woods hunt.

I look forward to when I can share the same thing with Jessie.

My Daughter the Hunter

I was finishing another magazine article when my daughter, Jessie, sidled up and stood next to me. Though only a first-grader, she understood about bothering Daddy when he was working. Jessie stood silently and watched the computer screen as I punched out the last sentences.

I typed every author's favorite words — "the end" — and then looked at my daughter.

"And what's on your mind today, young lady?" I said.

Jessie looked at me quizzically for several seconds.

"I was just wondering about something, Dad," she said. "I was just wondering if it's against the law for girls to hunt?"

For a split second, I didn't think Jessie was serious. But just as quickly, I realized she was. I'd learned from her older brother, Jake, that 6-year-olds don't ask anything but serious questions. I'd also learned they want serious answers.

I pulled Jessie onto my lap and looked her in the eye.

"No, it's not against the law for girls to hunt, Pumpkin," I said. "But whatever made you think it was against the law?"

Jessie's reply was immediate and eye-opening.

"Well, when I look through your hunting magazines, all I see is pictures of guys," she said. "And when I watch hunting shows on TV with you, all I see is guys on there, too. I just thought that I wasn't seeing any girls because it was against the law for them to hunt."

Jessie's Decision
I didn't discourage or encourage Jessie about hunting. I didn't dis-

"Don't say anything right away if you see a rub or scrape before I do," Jessie said. "Give me a chance to see it for myself first."

courage her because I wanted her to decide — and that's why I never had to encourage her. The day I assured her it wasn't illegal for girls to hunt, she decided to be a hunter.

Maybe it's not quite true to say that I didn't encourage Jessie. At every opportunity — which, in retrospect, wasn't often enough — I let her tag along in the woods. Through the years, she has been involved in spring and in-season scouting, shed-antler hunts, roosting turkeys and even baiting black bears in northern Wisconsin.

She has been a great companion — albeit unlike Jake.

A Different Personality
Jake was always content to walk behind and wait for me to point out interesting things. That's not true with Jessie. From the first

My wife, Geralyn, and daughter, Jessie, take in the sights at deer shows I attend. The way I see it, you couldn't put a future hunter in a more favorable environment.

day we hit the woods together, she wanted to lead.

"Just kind of tell me once in a while which way you want to go, Dad," she said. "And don't say anything right away if you see a rub or scrape before I do. Give me a chance to see it for myself first."

Of course, I obliged.

I'm sure Jessie would agree that she's learned much from our walks in the woods. However, I've also discovered a lot. For example, I learned immediately that Jessie prefers to lead, not follow. I also learned that she never stops talking in the woods.

Usually, her chatter involves questions. However, she also discusses school, friends, family or, if he's along, our black Labrador, Tok. Jessie gets a kick out of Tok's reactions when he momentarily loses track of us. He'll charge through the woods, occasionally bouncing high on his back legs, to spot us.

Invariably, Jessie's giggling gives us away.

A Great Environment

If you've seen me at a sports show, you've doubtless seen my wife, Geralyn. You've probably also seen Jessie. She loves attending shows, and we try to accommodate that. You couldn't put a potential hunter in a better environment. Incidentally, Jessie has proven her prowess with air guns many times at shows.

I remember when Jake accompanied me on his first hunt. Soon, Jessie will join me. Contrary to what some might think, I've never thought about how my hunting will suffer because, "I gotta take a kid in the woods with me." Believe me, I'll be privileged to experience that twice.

Yes, I'll have to make concessions. Jessie has already said she wants to hunt from a tree stand. However, I doubt she'll be comfortable at the height I typically place my stands. Further, there's the boredom factor. Every parent — hunting or nonhunting — knows about that. Children are easily bored, and mine are no exception.

Any time we spend with our children should be considered precious, so I don't care if my hunts with Jessie only last an hour. That's one hour I'll get to spend with her in addition to our regular family time.

There's something even more important. Experience indicates that children often develop special bonds with adults who take them hunting.

I don't doubt that I'll develop that special bond with my daughter.

Acknowledgments

This is always the most difficult part of my books to write, because the people who contributed to the final product are endless. I'm at a loss for words to express my sincere appreciation for their contributions.

However, a few people must be thanked by name for their assistance in making a book such as this possible.

First, I thank my lovely wife, Geralyn. Not once have you questioned me about what must appear to be an almost unhealthy obsession. I could cite many reasons for how I ended up where I am, but in the end, it all comes back to you. Your understanding and sincere respect for my passion for chasing big whitetails lets me realize my dream. I'm so glad you've stayed by my side and that you've shared my good fortune.

I must also thank my children, Jake and Jessie. Fulfilling my job obligations has made me miss an occasional football game, important school functions and even a couple of birthdays. You've never complained. I appreciate your understanding and love you more than you know.

Finally, I want to thank what I consider a great supporting cast: my mom and dad, and especially my brothers, Mike, Jim and Jeff. You've been instrumental in my success.

About the Author

Greg Miller was born and raised in west-central Wisconsin. He began gun-hunting for deer in 1964 with his father in the North Woods. He bought his first archery deer license in 1966. Even during those early years, Miller was passionate about chasing whitetails. That passion was tempered only because he didn't have a driver's license, which meant he couldn't hunt as often as he liked.

Some of Miller's fondest hunting memories occurred when he was considered a greenhorn. Though he didn't fill a tag during many of those hunts, Miller ranks them among his most memorable adventures.

Miller has hunted whitetails in several states, including Texas, Alabama, Georgia, Kansas, Nebraska, Missouri, Iowa, Illinois, Minnesota, Michigan, Montana, Wyoming and South Dakota. He has also hunted the Canadian provinces of Alberta, Saskatchewan and Manitoba.

Miller has shot some monster whitetails during his 30-plus-year career. Obviously, those hunts have provided him many cherished memories. However, as he always points out, the size of a buck's antlers have never — and never will — be his sole guideline for measuring the quality of a hunt or the resulting memories.

Miller lives in west-central Wisconsin with his wife, Geralyn, and children, Jake and Jessie.